THE

SUCCESS

PROJECT

10 Steps for the Mompreneur

Get Inspired
Write Your Story
Succeed at What Matters Most

www.TheSuccessProject.com

DL Publishing
420 North Twin Oaks Valley Road Suite 1873
San Marcos, California 92079

Cover Design – Paper Kite Designs
Photo - AcquaPhoto.com

ISBN 978-0692573020

For Madeleine, David, and Gavin. May your dreams be big and your faith be bigger.

Acknowledgements

To the women who lovingly contributed stories and experiences to this project, I thank you. After eighteen months of writing, I experienced my first real fear in this endeavor. The anticipation of this project's unveiling was unlike anything I've experienced before. But on my final read through, as I read over the list of names at the end of the book – the women whose stories are told here – a renewed sense of faith and comfort enveloped me. I visited each of your websites one by one and as I did so, I was reminded of how your stories so beautifully exemplify what this project is about. You inspire me and so many others. The effects of your project efforts are far-reaching. I am honored to share a piece of that magic with the world.

Contents

Note to Reader

I am honored that you decided to pick up this book. It is written directly to you, the project-starting mom - the mom who, like me, can't sit still - the mom who spends evenings conjuring up big ideas and nap times strategizing on how to make them fly. Somewhere along the lines you've recognized the creative magic that exists within you and you just can't let it rest. For many of us, *projects* are a creative outlet that can't be ignored. You and I are probably a lot alike and there are many others like us. Perhaps it's generational or just something in the water. Whatever it is, we *are* a generation of mothers who love to build projects. Whether you picked up this book because you're ready to pursue a burning idea, or you want to refine what you're doing already, I'm privileged to walk with you through this journey. It's one that I deeply cherish.

Just like any other project, this one began with a vision, but it eventually transformed into something else altogether. The Success Project was initially written as a tactical guide – the 10 steps necessary to get a home-based business up and running. With roughly 18 years of my own project-building experience, I recognized the pieces that are necessary to build a "successful" project and that was something that I wanted to share. For all intents and purposes, those elements still exist here. But when I finished my first manuscript, I recognized that something was missing. Not a little something... a huge, colossal something. This realization changed the direction of this book. In fact, it completely redefined the title, The Success Project. The word SUCCESS now represents something far more expansive. This experience was transformative, not just for the book, but for me personally. This would no longer be a tactical guide but rather, a manifesto of sorts.

So here is that big, colossal *something* that I recognized after my first read-through: *The person that I am writing to is YOU, the home-based mom and YOU are not the typical entrepreneur.* With that in mind, a *typical* approach to entrepreneurship would just be... futile. Believe me, I've experienced it first-hand. My family has endured living amidst project materials, emails have infiltrated my family time – I know what it's like to get buried by a project. The reality is, this *typical* approach to building projects can be devastating for a full-time mom. Our lives are multi-dimensional and our families are relying on us. You may volunteer in the classroom, work a part-time job, serve as a care-giver to a parent or a special-need child - but whatever those roles are, they have big implications. So, while this project will undoubtedly be a nifty new addition to your already-busy life, it's still... an *addition.* One more dimension among many.

For an entire year after making this grand epiphany, I delved in head-first in order to document the formula for creating a successful business and a thriving home life. During this process, I reached out to dozens of inspiring entrepreneur women who have done just that. I wanted to research their project histories, compare notes, document their experiences and pinpoint all of those great little details that every project-starting mom wants to know. After hours of interviews with lengthy discussion on this topic of "mompreneurship," I discovered commonalities among these women that could not be ignored: their approaches to project-building, their interactions with others, and the ways that they run their homes as they build their own businesses. As I delved deeper, I recognized that the process of building a successful project and creating a thriving home life are ultimately derived from the same place. In other words, both are produced by using the same formula. Furthermore, I recognized that the "creative outlet" that I so desire has a purpose. These projects aren't always just a fun side-note. In many cases, they're a source of purpose and influence.

After 18 months of research and writing, I give you the final product. The Success Project: 10 Steps for the Mompreneur reveals what I've discovered about building projects in the most meaningful way possible. It's everything that I wish I'd known from the start. From what I can see, these are the steps that are necessary to build a remarkable project while succeeding at what matters most.

Introduction

"A year from now you may wish you had started today."

--Karen Lamb

Mompreneur. It's a term that didn't exist 30 years ago. Some may consider it a catch phrase or just a clever nickname for a new trend, but if you're reading this, you know very well what it is. The fact is, "mompreneurship" is quickly becoming a recognized field within the small business sector. For the home-based mother, the breadth of possibility is expanding too quickly for me to quantify. With the help of the internet, it's now possible for the home-based mom to participate in a global market, in many cases, during a three-hour work day. This trend is tough to ignore. Around every corner seems to be a new face with a new creative brand.   Modern changes in technology have expanded our opportunities, diminishing that polarity between the working mom and the stay-at-home mom. We are living in a time when it's possible to be both. Modern changes in technology have transformed the face of business as we know it, creating industry that simply did not exist 30 years ago, industry that is highly compatible with the position of "full-time mom." Blogging, network marketing, online storefronts, podcasts, printable downloads... these are businesses that can be managed from the kitchen table. When it comes to home-based, money-making opportunities, the sky is the limit.

While this news is thrilling to many of us, let's not ignore the reality that mompreneurship is no cake walk. Mothers already have a vast spectrum of responsibility: taxi driver, tutor, councilor, cook, finance manager, housekeeper... not to mention, the heart of the home. So, add *business owner* to that list, and it's all likely to come unraveled. This is where approach is everything!

Drawing on my own experience and the expertise of dozens of inspiring entrepreneur women, I'm thrilled to present an approach to mompreneurship that produces more than a cool new business. In this system, the tactical aspect of project-starting and the process of producing a successful home-life are derived from the same place. This is where passion, purpose, and priority converge.

The Success Project is a title that is indicative of something much more than worldly "success." It is about cultivating the most important dimensions of our lives through worthy endeavors. Through our "projects" we can fortify those around us and discover a greater purpose for our own lives.

What We'll Cover

We'll start your Success Project from the very foundation in Phase I, *Charting the Course.* In STEP 1, we'll cover the most important ingredient. It's the key to living the life that you were meant to live! Through this first step, you'll realize what you should be doing and where you should put your time and your energy. If you've already started a business, this first step will help you determine whether you're headed in the right direction. This piece is presented first because it is absolutely the foundation. It should come before scheduling, research, and your game plan. When STEP 1 is applied, every area of life improves. It will be the key to producing the best possible project and the best possible life! Every other component presented in this book hinges on STEP 1.

In the following portion of Phase 1, we'll address your Success Project from the inside-out, delving into your mindset. How do you think? And how are your THOUGHTS influencing your experiences and your goals in life? And most importantly, how can you fine-tune your perspective in order to achieve a specific, desired effect? Mental planning is important for any project-starter, but for an entrepreneur mother, mental planning will determine the success of your life on many levels. During this step, you'll define exactly what you want and learn what's needed from YOU in order to achieve it.

Next, we'll cover the topic of organization in Phase 2 – *Building the Project.* This includes the secrets to maintaining a successful mom/boss schedule, ways to stay focused, and how to identify your top priorities. In this section, you'll learn to produce a maximum-work timetable that will encompass ALL of your current duties in life - those related to being a mother, a project starter, and anything else you have going! Through the expertise of several entrepreneur moms, we'll discuss ways to make it all work! During this phase of the program, you'll also learn to produce a clear and concise action plan for your project. This process involves brainstorming ideas and translating that vision into quantifiable, measurable goals. Then, we'll top off this phase by delving into actual project management to get your project off the ground.

In Phase 3, *Amazing, Fabulous You,* we'll look at your strengths, your weaknesses, and the *clutter* that may be holding you back. In this process, you'll discover that some of your habits are propelling you forward while others are restricting you. Most importantly, through this process, you'll learn to use your thoughts, words, and actions as a means to deliberate success.

In the final phase of your success project, *Pressing Forward,* we'll discuss challenges, ways to overcome obstacles, and ultimately, how to get this thing to the finish line!

My Assumptions about You

Before we begin, I'll admit to having a pretty concrete assumption about who you are as my reader. So here they are, my assumptions about you:

1. You are a woman who finds joy in your role as a mom. You realize that this time in life is precious. You're aware that many people rely on you. You're readily reminded that the years will pass by and that one day your kids will be grown. You want to make the most of your time with them.

2. You recognize things that inspire you and you have a sense for your ambitions. Perhaps you've had a burning idea or an opportunity to build your own private project. These sorts of things make you especially giddy!

3. The idea of setting your own schedule and making your own money is thrilling to you. You hope to translate your entrepreneurial passions into greater opportunities for yourself and the people that you love.

If these characteristics describe you, then you're a mompreneur by nature and you've got the right book!

How to Use This Book

The Success Project is a "PEN and PAPER READY" kind of experience. It includes various evaluative and planning exercises intended to guide you through the spiritual, creative, and strategic process of starting a business. These steps are based on key components that I discovered through my own experience and my research. I encourage you to work along in The Success Startpack, a resource provided at the back of this book and in printable format at my website: TheSuccessProject.com. The workbook provides corresponding activities that will help you identify your starting point, brainstorm your vision, and begin living a purposeful and joyful life. It might be helpful to read the entire book before completing the pages in the workbook.

Tools and Application

Before starting your project, it's helpful to first recognize that every learning process encompasses two fundamental dimensions: the tools and the application of those tools. In school, we recognize this as theory versus practice. It's the difference between learning what theoretically works, and then actually applying the skills in real life. You'll likely recognize some of the skills taught in this book, but perhaps you have never before applied them. This is the time to put those skills into action. That's what The

Success Project is all about! It's time to look at what you've been doing, decide where you want to go, and begin writing your own story.

I am committed to guiding you through this process! As we prepare to embark, take a moment to think of some of those well-known entrepreneur mothers. You've been introduced to many of them through Pinterest, Etsy, Instagram, and Facebook. They may write, or photograph, or cook, or design, but you know them because they've inspired you. They've taught you something that you didn't already know. They've imparted their wisdom, but most of all, their passion. It's by no accident that these women have reached us. It is only through proper use of time and vision that they've created something amazing and touched the world with their gifts. Through the same process, you can do it too. Now let's get started.

Phase 1 - Charting the Course

STEP 1

Get Inspired

"Men and women who turn their lives over to God will discover that He can make a lot more out of their lives than they can."
-Ezra Taft Benson

Inspiration is listed as the first step here because it is the foundation for every important decision that we make in life. It is effectively our means for understanding who we are and what we're here to do. You can learn where you're needed, what you should be doing, and how you can best fulfill your potential, as a mother, a project starter, a wife, a friend, and every other role that you hold in life! Inspiration is the key to it all. It is, unequivocally, the most important element for your success project! Yet, this component is so frequently overlooked. We often find ourselves searching for opportunities before seeking inspired direction, trying to guess what industries we're well-suited for and what project would be best for us. If you want to start this venture the *right way*, you must start by seeking inspired direction.

We've all heard business owners refer to this component as a "gut feeling" *You gotta go with your gut.* It's a common expression- but, I believe that the experience that they're referring to doesn't actually come from... the gut. It's not our instinct that guides us, but rather, a powerful divine source of wisdom.

To understand how inspiration works, you have to first recognize that all knowledge comes from the same great source. To put it simply, all true inspiration comes from God. When we prepare ourselves sufficiently, we can become tuned in to a world of knowledge! Inspiration not only leads to the correct path, it allows us to be successful in all of our inspired endeavors. Through this process, we begin to recognize our purpose in life and how we can best fulfill it.

The experience of receiving inspiration can't necessarily be described since it is so personal. For one, it might come through a feeling or a nudge in a particular direction. We might see something and recognize it as an inspiration or an answer to a problem. For me, it does often come in the form of a feeling inside of me. Other times, it feels as though someone just pressed the pause button - I can almost sense a moment of *did you get that? ...because it was important.* When we make a habit of recognizing and acting on inspiration, we get better at it!

We find it more and more and eventually, we learn to live each moment of our lives through this special gift.

In terms of your success project, think of inspiration as your instruction manual. This element will be your necessary resource for *paving the path*. Every project detail (from choosing a niche to scheduling and marketing) can be guided by this process. If it's something you're inspired to do, then you can be confident in knowing that the details will be revealed to you! When you are living through inspiration you can be assured that the most-important areas of your life will be accounted for as well. It is absolutely the "magic ingredient" to discovering your purpose, overcoming fear, and organizing the life that you were meant to live.

My Story

To illustrate how powerfully our lives can be shaped through inspiration, I'll share the story of my first success project with you. This experience changed the course of my life and taught me how to create an outcome collaboratively, through specific, inspired direction.

During the summer of 2002, I was preparing for my last semester of a bachelor's program. My daughter was three years old and we had planned the delivery of our second child to align with my upcoming graduation date. This point in my life represented the light at the end of a five-year tunnel. After years of juggling my education, work, and parenting responsibilities, my dream of being a full-time mom would finally be realized. I was elated at the prospect. Graduation was around the corner and my husband, Jamie had already begun an internship with a great company in the city. Life was sweet.

One afternoon at the end of that summer, I took my daughter to a local sandwich shop for lunch and a little bonding time. This otherwise-ordinary event would eventually prove to be the first of several life-changing experiences for me and my family. When I got to the front of the line to pay for our sandwiches, the cashier handed my check card back to me, "your card was declined." Declined!? In my mind, this had to be a mistake. Up until that day, I hadn't given much concern for our finances. We lived modestly, in a low-income apartment with just one car. A trust fund and student grants had paid for our education and our living expenses. But now we had Jamie's *real job*, with a *real salary*. Surely there was enough in our account for this ten-dollar lunch date.

There I stood awkwardly, sandwiches in hand, not sure what to do next. Hand them back? I asked the cashier to try my card again. No dice. A quick phone call to the bank confirmed my fears – "ZERO DOLLARS in your account." I took my daughter's little hand in mine and walked back home.

That night, Jamie and I reviewed our finances. After taxes, our new income was only a portion of what we'd previously lived on. How did we overlook this? But at this point, there wasn't much we could do. This was my new reality: We didn't have enough to get by. I was pregnant, I was scared, and in that moment, I was totally broke.

In tears, I walked outside to have a moment alone. I sat on a bench and sobbed. This is not how things were meant to be. And what did it mean? Me, finding a career after this new baby was born? What about my plan to be a full-time mom? With two children to care for and zero professional experience, I didn't see how this would possibly work. All I could do was cry.

At some point during the course of those long, relentless tears, I was interrupted by a strange and surprising glimmer of hope. In that moment, I suddenly pictured what my life would be like if my little family lived in one of the beautiful houses behind the gates around the corner. For a moment, I envisioned family nights and holidays in that house, a washer and dryer and our own garage to pull our own shiny car into. It's exactly the life that I pictured as a little girl. I wanted to be a grown-up mom with a beautiful grown-up house to raise my family in. And for a few seconds, I was reminded of that vision.

I suddenly felt a surge of determination to make that picture in my mind a reality. I gathered my composure and walked back into our apartment. Little did I know, I was about to embark on my very first success project.

Without a plan of any kind, I made it my intention to pay off our debt and move into the neighborhood next door. I prayed for direct guidance on the matter. I needed inspiration, an opportunity. How could we make the money we needed to get out of this place while maintaining my role as a stay-at-home mom? I was confident that *if* this was God's plan for me, I would find a way to achieve it. I immediately felt inspired in two ways. First, I needed to summon all of the gratitude within me. I realized that this was not the solution that I was looking for but rather, the preparation I'd need in order to receive inspiration. I wrote gratitude lists. I projected those feelings of gratitude toward my vision for the future. This experience alone was life-changing. Day after day, I discovered new things to be grateful for and as I did so, my enthusiasm for the plan escalated.

Next, I felt inspired to give a little extra in our monthly charity donation. It was counterintuitive. Yet, this physical gesture of faith was a way to prove to myself that I was committed to this plan. It also reminded me that there was enough in this world, enough for others and enough for me. I was confident that through these actions, an inspired answer would eventually come.

A few months went by. No changes or miraculous inheritance came, but instead, an idea. Jamie and I both felt the urge to go to real estate school. It didn't seem to fit the request I'd made to stay at home with the kids. And Jamie didn't have time to actually practice real estate either. But we went with it because we realized that somehow, it was an answer.

Roughly two weeks into the real estate course I had an epiphany. Jamie was at work and I couldn't wait to tell him. At the end of the day, when he walked through the door it was immediately apparent that he'd found the same answer. He blurted it out.

"We should go to Arizona where land is cheap and see if we can afford to buy a small investment property."

To this day we can't agree on who had the idea first. What we know for sure is that it came from the same place. This was the answer to our prayers. Real estate school led us to the solution that we needed. It was everything that I wanted and nothing that I expected.

Sixteen months after I'd cried on the bench, we sold our Arizona real estate investment and pocketed $150,000. We paid off our debt, made some investments, and moved into a house behind the gates. That is where we have since raised our family.

The approach used during that first experiment of FAITH has been duplicated through dozens of subsequent "projects" in my life. I have learned that whether it is a personal project, a goal for the family, or an entrepreneurial venture, we can be **inspired** to strategically design an outcome, ask for help, and receive the direction necessary to achieve it. Through this approach, projects are no longer an aimless stab at success. They each follow detailed specifications, outlined through divine inspiration.

The thing is, inspiration is everywhere. Possibilities, solutions, and answers to difficult problems - everything that we need. The key is recognizing them. When facing a tough situation that I need a resolution for, I often imagine a game of solitaire. I can't see the cards that are lying under each card pile, but God does. In any situation, He sees which moves to make. The key is getting tuned in so that we can see them too. If it is God's will for us, the necessary details will be revealed.

During my interviews for this project, inspiration almost always came up. Many of the women interviewed attributed their greatest successes to inspiration. Based on these findings, I've outlined the steps involved in the process of "getting inspired." From what I can see, these are things that we can do to maximize this essential component.

Ask

The first step to obtaining inspiration is to ask God. When you understand that all knowledge and wisdom comes from Him, you'll be inclined to ask for anything that you need. Whether it is social, political, familial, or personal, there is not a problem too complex for this process. Whether you need direction for a new project or a little redirection for a current project, you can receive inspiration by first asking.

Don't be afraid to ask with specificity! If you have an idea, submit it! See how you feel after asking. If you're on the right track, one answer will likely lead to another. Consider the outcome that you desire and pray for a way to achieve that outcome, if it is right for you. Consider the details of that ideal and include those in this process. This could include asking for ways to provide new opportunities for your family, an ability to give generously to others, or something else. When you ask for help in specific ways, you'll be more inclined to recognize the specific answers when they come.

Then, ask what is needed of you. Where should you be? What should you be doing? How can YOU best fulfill your potential?

In the international best-seller, and one of my all-time favorite books, "The Power of Positive Thinking," Norman Vincent Peale describes prayer this way: "Prayer power is a manifestation of energy. Just as there exist scientific techniques for the release of atomic energy, so are there scientific procedures for the release of spiritual energy through the mechanism of prayer."

BEAUTIFUL! The effects of prayer are miraculous and undeniable and although it is the most powerful tool, it is also remarkably simple. The effects of prayer can be experienced at the first try. It can be applied in the most simple or sophisticated circumstances. From finding a toy to building a business… there is not a problem too big for prayer.

When we try to navigate through life by ourselves, we inevitably miss some important moves. It's important to recognize that God may have bigger plans for us. In another favorite book of mine, "If Life Were Easy It Wouldn't be Hard," author Sheri Dew describes the experience of helping a friend hunt for a new house. As she prayed with her friend, Sheri asked the Lord to bless her with that house if it was His will… or something better. She writes: "It had never occurred to her to pray for 'something better' than she was imagining or conceiving. Yet none of us would wish to limit or restrain the Lord by the smallness of our vision or hopes or petitions....Is it possible that the Lord has blessings in mind for us---blessings and gifts and revelations so much better and knowledge so much greater than we have yet conceived, but blessings we haven't received because we don't ask. We don't petition. We don't plead."

What an insight! Just imagine what could be possible if we could utilize God's vision! The plans we hope for ourselves probably pale in comparison to what God has in mind. So, why not? Pray for what you want, *or something even better.*"

Pray for Desire

This concept initially swept me off of my feet. We often forget that we are not left here on our own. We can pray for a desire to accomplish the things that we're otherwise not capable of. Just imagine what could be possible if you could have the DESIRE for something. With this mind set, nothing is off limits. The introvert could pray for the DESIRE to be sociable, the disorganized could pray for the desire to be orderly, and the stubborn could pray for the desire to be flexible. You know those moments that you think, I'd love to start that business, but I'm just not, fill in the blank... a people person, organized, tech-savvy, whatever! The act of praying for desire helps us achieve the components that we don't already have. In terms of your project, recognize where you're falling short and pray for the desire that you need to make each area of your life work!

Listen for Answers

We can often find answers through the simple and subtle circumstances of life, a conversation with a friend or something heard in a talk, article, or lecture. As I began this book project, I engaged in countless conversations with friends that led me to what I should create here. While some were directly for the purpose of the book, other conversations had nothing to do with this subject. Yet, dozens of times during this writing process, I could almost hear a prompting to *just listen* to what my friends were saying. The answers are all around us – we just have to recognize them.

In order to listen, you must make your mind available for answers. When you need inspiration, quiet the distractions. Turn off the radio. Turn off your phone. Let your head rest and make room for inspiration.

This component was monumental for mompreneur, Andrea Tagalog as she sought for a better future for her family. During our interview she described her experience in building the company, PaleoBloks, and how "listening for answers" played in. Before her project began, Andrea felt particularly drawn to one of her talents: preparing delicious paleo meals. It was a niche that she'd become familiar with as a physical trainer. She loved the idea of starting her own Paleo meal-delivery system, but didn't have any idea how to get started. She knew that she needed inspiration on the matter. One day, during a physical training session, Andrea's client expressed her desire for home-delivered meals. The woman wanted to stay on the diet that Andrea had prescribed but was sick of eating bland, steamed vegetables at every meal. Andrea immediately recognized this as the inspiration that she'd been looking for. This was her opportunity to jump-start the paleo food delivery business. Through a series of subsequent inspirations, Andrea began to build her project. She secured a kitchen facility, made the right connections, and eventually established PaleoBloks. She knows that divine inspiration was the key to making it all come together. During my interview with Andrea she stated, *"You have to center yourself before you begin each day. Prepare yourself to receive the inspiration that you're looking for. Listen for the answers and then act on them."*

My dear friend, Susan, is another woman who built her project based on inspired direction. She had spent years working for the United States Postal Service before her children were born. After her first child, she switched to a graveyard shift so that she could be at home with the new baby during the day. The schedule soon became grueling. Although she was home, she felt exhausted and worn down from her nightly working hours. The graveyard shift couldn't possibly last forever for this new mom. After prayer and contemplation, Susan felt inspired to resign from her graveyard position. In a leap of faith, she knew that she'd find an inspired idea, something that would produce an income and allow her to be at home with her kids. Her answer did eventually come! It was through a friend who suggested that Susan take her knack for online resale to the next level. Intrigued, Susan asked for help. Her friend led her through the details of running an online resale shop. Within no time, Susan was producing the same cash flow that she had from the Postal Service while being a full-time mom to her kids.

When we are specific about what we need and faithful about the process, we can discover the tools necessary to make things happen! God sees all of the moving parts and will provide the best solutions if we will draw on that divine expertise.

Act

In order to receive inspiration, we must be willing to take action. This could mean researching, experimenting, or just asking questions. The point is, you're willing to do your part! Most of us have had the experience of losing a set of keys (or something else important) and then praying for help in finding them. It's something that readily happens in my house! We lose something, we pray for help, and then we look for it! We search everywhere. We lift up couch cushions, check under the furniture, hunt through cabinets and dresser drawers... until we find it. We don't sit and wait. We realize that in order to find something we've got to get out of our chair and look for it.

This seems like such a natural response when we're looking for a physical "something" that we've lost. Yet, it's so easily overlooked when we're looking for something less-tangible - an answer to a problem, say. But if we've asked for help in finding "something," no matter what it is, we must take action. Research, experiment, make phone calls, ask questions - do everything you can to get the answers. In this process of looking, realize that you might not find it in the first spot that you look. Just as you wouldn't give up after the first couch cushion, don't give up after the first few places. When you don't know where to go, it's important to start moving anyway. When you actively search for inspiration, you will find it.

Be Humble

The most common characteristic found in the women that I interviewed for this project was humility. Now I realize that this may not be a characteristic possessed by ALL business owners, but within the mompreneur business sector, this feature seems almost prerequisite. Every woman that I spoke to was generous with information, willing to discuss challenges, and each projected a sweet sense of encouragement for me in my book-writing endeavors. Upon interviewing each of these women, I realized that these characteristics were a result of their perspective. These women seem to know who they are. They recognize that they are the vehicle to something bigger than themselves. That perspective alone leads to inspired solutions in every area of life. If I were developing the shortlist of necessary characteristics for the entrepreneur mom, based on my interviews, HUMILITY would be at the top of the list!

There are a number of characteristics that seem to accompany this mindset. People who are humble don't seem threatened by others' successes. They have a greater sense of gratitude and they attribute their projects to something greater than themselves. It seems that when we humble ourselves, we become more available for answers. We open ourselves to not only the quiet whisperings of inspiration, but also to the people in our lives who provide solutions.

I have discovered that humility is actually a source of strength. And it makes sense. As humans we have a finite degree of knowledge. So placing faith in ourselves will always leave us feeling inadequate to some degree, no matter how smart we are. While some folks have been appropriately-deemed "experts" within their respective fields of "expertise," it's important to recognize that we are actually all just recipients of knowledge. RECIPIENTS. Meaning the knowledge that we HAVE doesn't come from within us. Paradoxically, as we humble ourselves to this knowledge, we actually become STRONGER, more knowledgeable, and more confident! Being humble isn't about being WEAK, it's about surrendering our inadequacies and opening ourselves to the immeasurable powers of God. In speaking to countless HUMBLE entrepreneurs, this quality does undoubtedly appear to be a key component in the project-building process.

Be Grateful

The longer that I live, the more I realize what a profound component GRATITUDE is to the process of getting inspired. We reap what we sow! It means that everything we put out is what we get back! So take a look at the opposing state of mind which is, of course, ingratitude. When we're not grateful, it's because we want more. So what seeds are we planting in that state of ingratitude? Scarcity? Inadequacy? Need? Those are certainly not things that anyone wants back! This is a fun topic, really. Because when you recognize it, it will change your life. Just imagine what the seeds of gratitude produce! Abundance, contentment, joy... We are directed in every necessary way when we humble ourselves in a state of gratitude. It opens our hearts and cultivates a sensitivity to inspiration.

Part of experiencing gratitude is, again, realizing that these things are not ours. Anything that I obtain (ANYTHING) is on loan. To feel a true sense of gratitude, I think we must first recognize that everything that we have is a gift for some greater purpose. When we come to this realization, we experience humility – the place where gratitude is rooted. Be grateful for what you already have and you will make room for more.

Prioritize

When beginning a project, it's tempting to succumb to a life of disarray on behalf of the new venture. Project materials take over the house. The television becomes the kids' new best friend. And ordinary duties are cast aside, all for the new cause - THE PROJECT! If this describes you in project mode, you are not alone!! This is typical, particularly for the creative mind! But here's the secret: when you complete the most-important responsibilities first, you will find that you are able to accomplish more everywhere, including your project. Why, you ask? Because, inspiration is most clear when life is in order. In order to get inspired, we must first prioritize!

I discovered this concept as I was knee-deep in a pretty time-intensive project. One day, as I sat at my computer, I experienced my first true writer's block. I could not produce a single sentence. I turned to research, looking for inspiration anywhere I could get it but still, nothing. After about an hour of standstill, I realized that the house had fallen apart around me. In that moment, I decided to finish my housework rather than sitting in this vortex of blank space.

I spent the following hour tidying up, folding laundry, wiping counters, and making beds, and during that process, something amazing happened. As I worked, I received profound inspiration for the project. PROFOUND! It was, in fact, the inspiration that I'd been searching for. I realized that the simple act of prioritizing (in that case, getting the house in order) made those lines of inspiration clearer and more direct. This experience changed my life. It made me realize two things:

1.   The value of TIME is actually less important than the value of inspiration.

2.   I wouldn't need 10 hours per day to make my big plan happen. I would only need to prioritize my life sufficiently to receive the inspiration that I needed.

This is, no doubt, one of the most important insights I've gained. It's a game changer! Prioritize your life according to the things that matter most, and you will be prepared for the inspiration that you need!

Serve Others

Taking time away from the project for the purpose of serving others feels completely counterintuitive when you're in project mode, but this is a key component for a few reasons. First off, there is just a sort of magic that exists in the realm of "service." It's not the same as work. While work depletes you, service has more of a replenishing effect. When we serve others, the windows of inspiration seem to open wide and time seems to be on our side. By dedicating more of ourselves to people in need, we maximize our efforts in every area of life. This is a concept that's tough to prove. It's something that you must experiment with in order to see the effects.

I was first introduced to this concept by a friend who shared an experience with us. He had been asked to volunteer at a local food bank on the same day that he was preparing for a speech that he was to deliver the next day to a group of Spanish-speaking members of our church. He thought he needed to spend the entire day working on the talk because his Spanish was rusty, but knew the volunteer work was important as well. Although he felt as though he didn't have time to squeeze it in, he went to the food bank anyway – he knew that's where he needed to be.

That visit to the food bank proved to be the best-possible decision in more ways than one. During a conversation with a fellow food bank volunteer he learned of a new technology which had just hit the Internet: Google Translator. It was a complete epiphany to him. Later that day, he was able to write his talk in a short period of time thanks to that newly-discovered translation tool. His point in sharing this story was to illustrate how profoundly we find answers when we are willing to serve others.

As I spoke with world-renowned photographer and mompreneur, Jill Thomas, she echoed these sentiments with one of the most compelling stories I've ever heard. She first explained that "getting outside of yourself" is a key element for anyone hoping to get inspired for a project. She then shared this incredible story: In the early years of Jill's photography career, she was asked to volunteer her skillset for a very special occasion. For this particular event, the people involved couldn't otherwise afford a photographer. Although she had little experience in this realm of photography, she pulled together the ideas and resources to make it happen. Not long after the photoshoot, one of her images was featured on the cover of a widely-known wedding magazine. As you can imagine, this put Jill's new business "on the map" in one of the most competitive industries around. To this day, the pristine photographic artwork of Jill Thomas can be found in countless magazines and websites around the world and her unique photography style has influenced much of this industry on a whole. It all began when Jill was willing to volunteer a few hours on a Saturday afternoon to some people in need.

The more I experiment with this component, the more I recognize the undeniable effects of service. It does INDEED lead us to the answers we need, lending us better experiences, more time in our pockets, and a more-effective approach to making things happen! Start each day by asking God where you're needed and realize that service opportunities will bless your life and your project efforts!

Recognize Inspired Opportunities

Opportunities are all around us: opportunities for change, influence, and to make a difference in the world. Inspiration is the key to recognizing it. Then, we must be willing to take action! When we respond to inspired opportunities, something truly amazing happens.

When Andrea Faulkner Williams returned home from an 18-month religious mission for her church, it was difficult transitioning from her life as a full-time missionary back into the woman that she once was. She soon realized that she was not alone in this experience. Over time, she met countless other returned missionaries that were experiencing the same challenging transition. Andrea recognized the opportunity in front of her! She recognized that other women needed support. They needed a place to turn for advice and experience. As a means to share her own story and offer support to other returned missionaries, Andrea authored the book, *Tell Me About it, Sister - A Guide for Returned Sister Missionaries*. A simple willingness to recognize and act on opportunity caused Andrea to fulfill a purpose in her own life and to uplift and support others.

Mother/entrepreneur team, Lauren Foulger and Erica Smart were inspired by an opportunity to create change for the remote, humble villages of Guatemala. As Lauren worked there with the World Health Organization, she experienced first-hand the cycle of poverty that exists in the world. During that time, she recognized a great need for the families there as she witnessed mothers with no way to provide for their starving children. Lauren wished she could institute some kind of change for these humble villagers. She would soon find her answer, joining forces with Erica Smart, a successful entrepreneur who shared her love for humanitarian work. The two combined their passions for style with their desire to create change. They co-founded Humble Hilo. The philanthropic handbag/apparel company brings Guatemalan textiles to modern fashion. Handbags, dresses, and shoes are humbly made by the native village people. Inspired, no doubt, the Humble Hilo team established industry through these native crafts, streamlining a portion of the product revenue back to the people of Guatemala. The project extends this humanitarian experience directly to their customers, in an effort they've entitled: Pick a Project. At checkout, buyers can decide which effort their purchase will support: child nutrition, women's literacy, or a microcredit loan for women in Guatemala. On the Humble Hilo website, Lauren writes:

"After holding and weighing one malnourished baby after another... I left heartbroken and determined to do anything I could to help break the cycle of poverty. I am humbled and beyond grateful seeing the change that is happening because of your help. When we say thank you for your support, we sincerely mean it on behalf of us and so many others."

What a beautiful and profound example of seeing and acting on opportunity for change. It makes me wonder how many opportunities have flown by unnoticed. I believe that when we're ready to receive inspiration, we'll no-doubt see the opportunities that we are each uniquely prepared for! God can work through each of us, if we are willing to recognize the need and use our talents and resources to produce solutions.

Wrapping Up

As you plan, let inspiration be your guide. Regardless of where you are on your project journey, it's never too late to institute this component. Ask for help and prepare yourself for answers; through this process you can become the vehicle to whatever great endeavors you are inspired to pursue. Inspiration is always, ALWAYS, the first step. When you're inspired, you can find the best and quickest ways to solve problems and you can receive specific direction on how to build your project! Regardless of your current situation, you can find out what to do next.

Ways to help you get inspired:

- Ask
- Listen for answers
- Act
- Be Humble
- Be Grateful
- Prioritize
- Serve Others
- Recognize Opportunity

STEP 2

Set Your Intention

"Rise up and become the person you were meant to be."
-Dieter F. Uchdorf

Intention is exciting. This is the portion of the project that puts you in the position of the author. You are here to write your story. Now is the time to ask this important question. *Where do you want to be in 5, 10, and 20 years from now?* Give it a moment. Picture yourself, your family, your living conditions – picture all of it. That picture of what you want is your intention.

Stephen Covey referred to this component in terms of "beginning with the end in mind." Up until this point, dreams and ideas may have floated in and out of your mind. You may have thought, *oh, that's a great idea, I should get on that.* But until you set a deliberate intention, those ideas will go right on floating. Your current intention may be to start a new product line, write a book, enter a direct marketing business, or something else. When you set a deliberate intention, you clearly see what you're after and you see how it will effect your life. You commit to it! If it's something that God also has in mind for you, then you're about to experience quite a ride. Setting an intention is like opening the windows of inspiration and saying, *I'm ready to collaborate. I'm committed, let's go.*

While the word INTENTION is commonly used, the context that we're speaking of may be something quite different than what you're used to. DELIBERATE INTENTION is a meaningful, faith-based objective for some particular outcome. When you use this step correctly, your intention becomes the catalyst to a series of, often unforeseen, circumstances leading to your outcome. The magic begins when intention is formed through the process of inspiration. Through this approach, you will receive all of the necessary components to bring the idea to life. You are not working independently OR waiting for things happen, rather, you are drawing on the wisdom of God in order to build your masterpiece.

While inspiration is the foundation, it only works when put into action. Intention is our active part. We must see what's needed and strategize a course of action. In "my story" mentioned earlier, inspiration was certainly the foundation. But the experience began with my *intention* to change my situation. I believe that, as humans, we're entitled to this experience of strategizing, designing a solution, and receiving the inspiration we need to make it happen. I've experienced it first hand, and I've spoken with countless mompreneurs who have experienced it as well. Whether your intention is to create a thriving home life, better eating habits, or success in your new project venture, decide what you're going for and commit to it! That's how it begins.

Identification

Identify what you want. Be prayerful during this process. You should feel confident in knowing that this is a good desire - one that will positively influence your life and the lives of others. For now, don't get caught up in the details of HOW it will come about; for now, just decide what you want.

During my first Success Project, my intention was to move into a house behind the gates. I had no idea how I would earn enough money to do that, but I set a precise trajectory. That landing place included a few specific details, namely, to continue my self-appointed role as a stay-at-home mom WHILE earning the money that we needed to move into a house. I eventually saw the details, the first step was to simply identify my intention.

Don't fret over whether or not you're qualified for this endeavor. Inspiration is the only qualifying factor necessary! Identify what you want and commit to it. This is your agreement to start the collaborative process.

If you haven't already started a project, knowing WHAT to do can be one of the most challenging aspects of this process. You may want to find that "landing place" but don't yet know what that is. In that case, draw on things that interest you. What are you curious about? What are the things that you're drawn to? What do you enjoy? Think about your interests, your talents, and your calls to greatness. These may be things that you currently pursue, or perhaps they're the things that you've always wanted to pursue. What calls to you? For some of us, a deep, enduring fondness for humanitarian work may be present, for others it may be a love for organization, conversation, writing, or design. Think about those things that interest you and realize that it is by no accident that you feel a desire for these experiences. You have a unique potential for influence. This is where your purpose lies! When you feel drawn to something, don't ignore it!

Mompreneur, Heather Balliet has built an incredible business that stemmed from her love for parties. As a little girl, Heather loved to plan little parties, play dress, up, and create beautiful things. After planning her own wedding, she realized that this natural talent for design could potentially work as a business. Heather formed Amorology, a full-service event coordination and design company. In a relatively short period of time, Heather's passion for design translated into a successful business. Amorology's events have been featured by Martha Stewart Wedding, Bride Magazine, and many other high-end media venues. The company is followed by tens of thousands through Instgram and Pinterest. Through her passion, Heather has touched the lives of countless people. As we discussed this topic in our interview, Heather emphasized the importance of this component by describing how our passions are the things that we'll become good at. She explained that when we love doing something, we invest more of ourselves. We should pursue the things that we love.

In an interview that I watched YEARS back, a motivational speaker explained that you can be absolutely GREAT at anything that you love. It didn't take long for this concept to really resonate with me! If it's something that you love, pursue it! Even if it's something that you're interested in, pursue it! Play with it. Entertain it. See what happens! When you do what you love, people are drawn to you! Blogging is a perfect example of this concept. No one ever said, *I really want to start reading about how a mother of five gets her kids to do chores in the midst of crazy life*. But countless mommy-bloggers have reeled in millions of readers to talk about those very things. The market didn't demand it... they simply showed us something that we liked, and we responded. When you do what you love and do it well, people will follow you.

When Katie Sabin opened an Etsy craft shop in 2013, she had no idea that her Instagram following would soon skyrocket to TENS of thousands of followers. Katie was doing something that she enjoyed: crafts! She had begun the hobby as a distraction from the rewarding (yet often monotonous) life as a mother to TWIN BOYS! That hobby quickly developed into a periodic "craft night" so that she could share this pastime with her friends. Her motive was never to make a career of it... she was simply doing something that she loved. As she shared crafting highlights over Instagram, her followers simply fell in love. Before long, Katie was featured on the cover of a nationally published craft magazine. She didn't set out for it, it simply happened as a result of pursing something that she loved.

A similar experience also transpired for blogger and decorating extraordinaire, Shelley Smith. Her blog began as a way to track the cosmetic progress of her home remodel. As she posted stunning photo updates on her blog, the world took notice. Before long, "The House of Smiths" blog became a web sensation. Pinterest posts went viral and followers everywhere were soon using the blog as a resource for their own remodeling projects! Shelley's site has become a household name for bloggers everywhere. It started from something simple: her talent for writing and her love for decorating and remodeling. It's certainly blossomed into something much bigger! The following quote appears at HouseofSmiths.com:

"Blog about what you love, have no regrets and aim for the overall goal to leave people feeling more motivated, inspired, and happier than when they came."

I believe that we can discover our passions by simply leaning into the things that spark an interest. Pay attention to the things that you're curious about. Spend a little time with them! That's where you'll find it.

Motivation

Once you've identified WHAT you want, you should begin to think about your motivation for this endeavor. In other words, why do you want it? When it comes to the pursuit of any endeavor, the WHY is actually more important than the WHAT. We don't do anything "just because." We do things for a reason. That REASON is our motive. It's the thing that keeps us going even when things get tough. So we must understand what that driving motive is for the goal at hand. Why do you want it? Is it for honor, prestige, financial success, survival, or perhaps something else?

For a moment, just consider some of the driving motives that already exist for you. Take your role as a mother for example. Why do you get up early to make breakfast for your kids even when you're exhausted from a sleepless night? Why do you wipe boogers, wrangle them into the bath, enforce a consequence, or play Candyland for the 20th time? Are these experiences that we desperately love? Are they a source of immediate joy? I guess I'll let you answer that for yourself. But from my perspective, we do many of these things because we LOVE our kids. Even when we get tired, grumpy, or emotional, the love that we have for them drives us to do our best. When it comes to our kids, LOVE is the solid motive. When this kind of iron-clad motive comes into place, our activities shift from a matter of happenstance to a fixture of conviction and necessity.

Just imagine if other areas of your life were supported by such a solid, driving force. As we think about our projects we must consider our motivation for them. Think again about WHY you want the thing that you want. What is it? Is that motivation something worth fighting for? Is it a motive that will drive you even when you're tired, busy, or feeling uninspired.

If the motive isn't good enough, then the endeavor will fizzle out. This happens every time you start a project and fall off. We must understand what our motives are and more importantly, we must believe in them.

Sometimes, when things aren't working out, it's due to a disharmony between the GOAL and the MOTIVE. In fact, you might be resisting the outcome because you don't feel good about achieving it. The pursuit of *losing weight* is a great example. For many people, the dream of having a "perfect body" is coupled with unconscious concerns related to pride, unwanted attention, or attracting the wrong things. For some people, a self-defeating weight loss process ensues when the core motive is *to look hot.* Often times, *successful* weight loss is preceded with a shift in motive. When a person's motive changes from *looking hot* to something much bigger, say, *a desire to be around for the grandkids*, then the goal becomes attainable. It's more worthy of fighting for. The goal hasn't changed. Only the motive has changed.

This example can likewise be extended to your goals related to money, happiness, or your success project specifically. For most people, the desire for money comes from a desire for opportunity. But often times, fear of power, pride, greed, and selfishness get in the way of our pursuit for money. These are true concerns because, frankly, the pursuit of wealth can destroy lives when the motives are not correct. But in reality, financial success can also serve the purpose of enhancing life experience. In other words, it can bless our lives when used the right way. When we aim to make money from THIS perspective, our financial endeavors will be more successful. Again, it's all about that MOTIVE, WHY we're doing the things that we do!

The good news is, you can always reconsider your motives, or as my dear friend, Amie White says, "purify" them. Purify your motives! What a beautiful concept. It means to look at your goals and identify the best reasons for accomplishing them! Draw on your core principles during this process and determine whether or not your motive is in alignment. Once you've developed a sincere motive toward any particular goal, you can achieve it.

As I began writing this book in 2014, I was initially intrigued by the idea of accomplishing such a seemingly noble goal. I'd spent some time in the content development field and realized that all of my hundreds of hours in writing could, instead, be channeled into something that I was actually passionate about: *project-starting*. I decided to write a book that would help other moms who wanted to start a business from home. My motive was to help people, and that seemed pretty good to me. But in November of 2014, that motive became something much bigger. It happened when I bumped into a woman that I have revered for much of my adult life.

She is a speaker, a leader, and an author. Her name is Elaine Dalton. When I saw her in a local restaurant, I was ecstatic and a little star-struck. I have listened to all of her talks and interviews. I am definitely one of her biggest fans. As she walked passed me, I leaned toward her and decided to make my move: *"Hi Elaine. I would not be more excited if Oprah Winfrey were standing in front of me right now."* -Yeah, really. Elaine's response could not have been more perfect. Her beautiful face beamed as she looked me squarely in the eyes. She told me how impressed she was by a generation of women who were leading the way, setting an example, and using their talents to inspire good in others. She had no idea what I was up to, but I felt as though her words were intended just for me. That brief conversation made me completely rethink what I was doing and even more so, why I was doing it. It enlightened my mind to a greater purpose, a motive that I knew my Heavenly Father would be proud of: to share what I've learned about the power of *inspiration*. That element would no longer be just an ingredient in the recipe of project-building. It would become the centerfold of this approach: *To teach others how God can direct every aspect of our lives, even our projects.*

Let's now take a look at your goals for your new project. Think about this. What is your motive? Why do you want it? Is it for the purpose of helping others? Is it for prestige? Honor? Health? Recognition? Survival? As you look at your goal, determine the most important reason for achieving it. Develop a motive that God will be proud of. Ask yourself:

What do I want?

Why do I want it?

The answers to these questions should make you feel good. They should bring up a feeling of passion and excitement! The heart of this program is to enable you to achieve great things without leaving out the important stuff... your people, your influence, and your mark on the world. By simply identifying what you want, and defining a corresponding PURE motive for that particular endeavor, you'll begin to route a truly successful plan.

Declaration

Once you have identified what you want and you recognize WHY you want it, declare your intention. This portion of the plan represents your commitment to the process. You haven't just thought about it... you're ready to make it happen. It's a lot like making an order in a restaurant. If you have the intention to order a Cobb salad for lunch, you will likely tell your server that you're going to have a Cobb salad. As long as she hears you, and the kitchen is prepared to make a Cobb salad, that's exactly what you'll get. The operative step here is the ordering process itself. You've *declared* what you want to eat. Once you've made that order, the kitchen team and the servers will collaborate in order to make your "Cobb salad" dream a reality.

Just think about wanting something, but never ordering it. You might have instead said to the server, bring me something that tastes good... something with vegetables and a tasty dressing. I suppose there's a chance you'd get a Cobb Salad, but it's not as likely. See, thinking vaguely about what might taste good isn't going to produce what you really want for lunch. You have to decide what it is exactly and make your order. That's when it will happen.

This declarative process can be applied to goals related to family life, your business, or any other endeavors you have going on. Whatever it is that you're going for, make a concerted decision about it. It's no longer an idea floating around. This is something that you're committed to. You've prayed for it, you feel good about it, and now you've entered an agreement with the process. That's when the necessary elements will start to work together. That's when it will happen.

Amplify Your Intention

Like anything else in life, it takes practice to maintain a state of deliberate intention. When we want to achieve a particular outcome, the first step is to pray for it. If it's in our best interest, then something magical begins. Not magical in the sense that it all happens immediately. In fact, there will be work entailed. But there is something truly miraculous about this process. Unseen forces seem to work together to bring the inspired endeavor to life. For me, this experience often feels like a roller coaster. When you get into the right cart on the right track, it takes off. You feel things happening that you know you couldn't have created on your own. There are passes and turns that you could have never expected, but they're all leading you to where you want to go.

Through the years, I've heard so much discussion about how to make this process more powerful. Prayer is unequivocally the most powerful step. Writing it down is a component that reminds us of what we've committed to. Here are some other powerful steps that I've learned through the years to help make that intention more powerful.

Visualization

The effects of mental imagery have been noted by countless business owners and Olympic athletes. Multiple studies have concluded that mental practice can be nearly as effective as physical training. Researchers and psychologists have noted that mental imagery impacts cognition more than we've previously realized. Our perception, motor planning, and memory are influenced by visualization, yielding overall improvement in motor performance, motivation, and confidence.

In terms of your project, visualization is a monumental piece! Gymnast and Olympic gold-medalist, Peter Vidmar, described his experience with visualization when training for the summer 1984 Olympics in a youth seminar that I attended in 2013. Vidmar described his mental preparation technique that eventually translated into a gold-metal victory. During his Olympic training days, Vidmar regularly rehearsed his gymnastics routine in his mind. He imagined a perfectly executed routine - going through every motion, every step, just as if he were performing the routine in real life. He made a habit of running through this mental exercise every day. He DID eventually execute his routine perfectly. In 1984, Vidmar scored a perfect 10 on his pommel horse routine. It's one of very few perfect scores in Olympic history.

Visualization was also a key element in my first success project, mentioned earlier. During a long stretch of time, I actually had no idea how to achieve my vision but each day I created a picture of it in my mind! I did it until that experience was real for me. I knew that it was achievable and that it was only a matter of time and inspiration.

Here's how to visualize:

- Create an image of what you want to achieve, as if you've already achieved it. Close your eyes and imagine that moment as if it's already happened or is presently happening.

- Create detail in that moment. For instance, imagine the way you're dressed and the way you see the people/things around you.

- Experience the emotions you're feeling in that moment that you're creating. Create a sense of gratitude for what you imagine you've achieved. Feel those emotions each time you visualize. When you bring up feelings of longing or wishing, you're in the wrong place. Instead, bring up feelings of contentment and gratitude as if you're already living in that desired experience.

- Experience the senses. Imagine the sounds and smells associated with the moment you're creating in order to make this image as real as possible.

- End your visualization with a lingering state of contentment and gratitude. You should feel SO content that any sense of longing is gone.

Visualization is fantastic way to prepare for an anticipated event: a talk or speech, a proposal, or even a daunting interview. I visualize every time I have to sing a solo in front of a large group. Let me be clear: I'm only a soloist when you don't have a soloist. But sometimes I'm asked and I won't say no. This particular visualization exercise is useful when fear is involved! It's sort of a step-1/step-2 process that allows you to create the event without the associated fear. It's a dress rehearsal of sorts. Here's how it works: Start by closing your eyes. Then, imagine the event as if you're watching a movie. This is a great way to approach a situation that you're nervous about because... It's only a movie. Watch that event transpire in your mind from beginning to end with someone else playing YOU, the main character. Once you've seen the event unfold in the manner you've created, then rethink the event as the main character. You're no longer watching the movie. This time, you're recreating the scenario from start to finish but this time, YOU are in the scene! Remember the detail as you're walking through the event. Rehearse the event EXACTLY the way you expect to experience it in real life. You'll be amazed to see how real life responds to this powerful visualization exercise! It's the ultimate preparation technique.

In order to effectively visualize, you must first have those concrete details as discussed in the identification phase. Imagine the people around you and the feelings that you have in that moment. This is an absolutely powerful exercise!

The Bucket List

Pretty simple. Form a list of everything you want to accomplish or experience. Items on your bucket list can be as practical or extravagant as you can imagine. Your list should include experiences that you hope for. That may include vacations, humanitarian activities, creative projects, family experiences, career goals... anything that you want before you die, LIST IT. Let the world around you be your guide. Nothing is off limits.

After about 12 years of marriage, my husband and I found a journal from his first year in college. He had a bucket list written in the back page. The book was stored in a box of memorabilia that he hadn't looked at in all 12 years of our marriage. As we read through the list, we were astonished to see how many items could now be check-marked. These goals were specific! It was truly amazing to see how closely the events of his life echoed the items of this old bucket list while he had totally forgotten about it! Life responds when we simply formalize our intention!

Add to your bucket list throughout your life. When you see things or experiences that you desire, tack them to your list! When my grandmother passed away, I spent a few weeks with my extended family up in Oregon. During that time, I noted a few of my aunt and uncles' family traditions and recognized them as experiences that I wanted to provide for my own family. When I got home, I added those traditions to my own bucket list.

As you keep this going through the years, you'll be amazed to see the events of your bucket list materialize.

The Vision Board

A vision board is a great tool, particularly when it comes to projecting an intention with visual detail. The idea is to simply select and paste images that represent your vision and then display them as a reminder of your intention. A friend of mine had the intention of completing medical school so she mocked up a medical school diploma with her name and placed it on vision board. Other ideas can include checks, photographs of landscapes, vacation destinations, or bold-print phrases that capture the *vision*. Physical images often evoke enthusiasm, joy, and deep emotional response, reminders of what we're after and better yet, WHY we're after it.

If you choose to represent your intentions through a vision board, or perhaps through framed pictures or quotes, make sure to put them where you're see them daily! Visual reminders can take the form of a screen saver, a picture on your phone, or even a Pinterest board. Let these pictures serve as a reminder of where you're going and WHAT you will achieve.

Verbal Affirmations

Another approach to amplifying your intention is to declare your vision out loud, as if you've already achieved it. This is called a verbal affirmation. The idea is to program the mind, convincing oneself of what is possible. In an article entitled, *The Wise Open Mind* Psychologist, Ronald Alexander Ph.D., states:

The mind doesn't know the difference between what is real or fantasy. When you watch a movie and you start to laugh or cry your mind is empathizing with the characters on the screen even though it is only Hollywood magic.

In the same way that our minds can be tricked into feeling grief, excitement, fear, or happiness for a character in a movie, we can likewise *trick* the mind into believing that something is achievable. As humans, we have a miraculous way of solving problems. The reticular activating system is a part of the brain that collects and filters information. In essence, this is our involuntary means for deciding which information is necessary to any given situation. When you're driving a car, this part of your brain allows you to tune certain things out, while paying attention to things that are pertinent to your experience as a driver - sirens, stops lights, horns, turning signals. The reticular activating system provides a way to filter out all of the unnecessary information so that you can perform well in whatever you're doing. Now here's how verbal affirmations play in. If you create a scenario and verbalize it as if it's true, that scenario becomes believable to the mind. Then, the reticular activating system will provide the information necessary to make that scenario true.

Here's a fun way to experiment with this process: Create an affirmation that changes or magnifies your feelings toward a person in your life. You might, for instance, say, "*I love and cherish my husband who I am deeply attracted to.*" Do this several times a day and you will experience a profound change in that relationship! Your Reticular Activating System will filter the things that are bothering you and instead SHOW YOU all of the reasons that you LOVE and CHERISH your husband! It sounds crazy but it works!

This experience of reciting daily affirmations can be very powerful when coupled with the corresponding state of gratitude. When you declare a desired experience as something you're grateful for already achieving, you send a powerful message to your mind! That positive state of gratitude will accelerate your intention! When creating an affirmation:

- Choose positive words. Rather than describing what you're NOT or what you don't want, create affirmations that are descriptive of what you want exactly.
- Speak your affirmations out loud.
- Speak in present tense, as if the experience has already happened. If you begin an affirmation with the phrase "someday..." then you'll feel a sense of longing or wishing rather than gratitude and contentment.
- Write your affirmations out first before saying them out loud.

The Road Map

The Road Map was a requirement during the last semester of my husband's executive MBA program at University of Southern California. The assignment required each student to produce a map representing the events of his or her entire life in pictures: from birth until his death. The thrilling part of this exercise is, of course, planning the future, deciding everything you want to do before you die! Luckily for me, I was able to participate in this Road Map project. Together, Jamie and I decided that we wanted to live by the beach after we retired. We included places that we wanted to travel, humanitarian missions, and grandchildren. Jamie printed out pictures to represent each of these events in his life. Any time now, he can return to that project and include new items! It's a powerful exercise and another visually detailed expression of intention.

When I served as president of the Young Women's organization at my church, I planned a picture road-map activity for each new school year. I encouraged the girls to think about their talents, things they wanted to explore, school goals, and relationships in their families. Then, they each cut and pasted pictures that represented those goals.

Visual declarations serve as a great reminder during the beginning phases of your project or during the ebbs and flows of success. When you face discouragement or doubt, the images found there remind you of your ambitions and help you stay focused to your course.

The Journal

Journaling is a cathartic and purifying way to create and maintain intention. And bonus... it creates an instant record of your experience. Through a regular routine of writing, some people are able to best-identify areas in need of change, and to track their progress. It's a fantastic reminder of how far you've come.

Using your journal to track your success projects can be a great choice for several reasons. First and foremost, it allows you to lay out all of your goals on paper and include specifics regarding your vision, your search for inspiration, and your action plan. My journal includes many of my life's success projects including businesses, life action plans, and changes to current projects. It's a remarkable experience to record very specific details and later see them come to fruition. It certainly increases your trust in the process as well as your sense of gratitude.

Journals can likewise be excellent teaching tools to later generations. As we document our struggles, our ability to overcome, our goals, and our achievements, our posterity will one day see how it was done!

The Physical Contribution

Clear out a space for new client documents. Test drive the car of your dreams. Increase your charity donation. Walk the grounds of a future build-out. These are all ways to make your intention REAL for yourself. For some, a physical expression can be a powerful tool in the creative process. It's a confirmation to the mind that you are confident and may consequently magnify your intention.

A physical contribution may also include displaying a physical symbol that reminds you of your goal. For a young, aspiring ballerina, a pair of professionally-worn toe shoes is a physical reminder of her desire to work for the ballet. For a young baseball player, it's an MLB baseball mitt. For me, a picture of the building where my husband and I were married signifies the commitment that we've made to our family and to God. Seeing that picture reminds me of where I'm headed and subsequently, the actions that are necessary to make a successful marriage. Just like the vision board or the verbal affirmation, a physical contribution encourages the mind to focus on what's necessary to make that event really happen.

Cultivation

Cultivation is the final phase and the determining factor in the process of intention. This part is monumental. In order to understand how it works, you've got to first realize how paramount your MINDSET is. That is where cultivation takes place.

If you were planting a seed, you know that it would need water, nutrient-rich soil, and sunlight in order to blossom. Those are specific requirements in order for that seed to grow. The cultivation phase of intention is no different. Just like the process of planting a seed, you can harvest the experiences that you desire by cultivating specific corresponding thoughts and actions.

It's easiest to understand in terms of negative and positive outcomes: *When we plant seeds of negativity, we produce negative experiences - when we plant seeds of positivity, we produce positive experiences.* But in reality, this principle is much more specific. We cultivate precise experiences based on the seeds that we sow. Consider the seeds of generosity, gratitude, faith, hopefulness, praise, charity... imagine what experiences they cultivate. For every action and state of mind there exists a corresponding fruit. In order to produce that fruit, we must plant the right kind of seed.

Now, consider this: without deliberate cultivation, we may inadvertently produce the wrong kinds of experiences. Many times, this happens as a result of our negative habits. For example, when you set an intention to start a new business, but then dwell on how busy and exhausted you are, you find yourself busier and more exhausted than ever! Why? Because you're cultivating a state of being busy and exhausted. It's become a habit. We're all guilty of this from time to time. It's important to periodically take check so that negative thoughts, words and actions don't become the source of the harvest.

You might be starting new projects and wondering why they're not lifting off. A little introspection may be in order! It's possible that you're giving attention to the wrong things and as a result, you're getting the "wrong things" back.

When you set an intention for something, you've got to feed that intention. Believe that it's possible. In other words, be faithful. Don't ever say something that you wouldn't want to be true - *This is never going to happen. I'm just innately too disorganized to run a business...* Whatever those thoughts are, recognize them. Don't contradict your vision by putting yourself down. When you feel fear based on comparisons to others, recognize them and change your thought process. Make a CHOICE about how you think, speak, and act! Practice positive thought patterns in order to cultivate your vision and make it true.

We will talk more about cultivation in STEP 8 and delve into specific habits that may be holding you back. For now, just recognize that our thought patterns are very-much connected with the existence that we're creating. Any new project, goal, or change in life begins with a willingness to set an intention, declare it, and properly cultivate it.

True Stories of Intention

One of my favorite stories of deliberate intention comes from entrepreneur, Collette Larsen. The mother-of-five was emotionally ravaged after her youngest daughter's life ended due to cystic fibrosis. In a state of devastation, Collette also faced a difficult, continuing reality. With no career and little money, the single mother still had four children to support including another child with Cystic Fibrosis, Sharlie. At that time, Sharlie was given just one year to live. Collette needed a game plan. She needed to make money quickly, while continuing her role as a stay-at-home mom so that she could continue to care for her sick child. She would do everything she needed to support her family and to keep Sharlie alive. She had a dream but she needed a vehicle - a business that she could run from her home. She turned to a company in the network marketing industry - USANA Health Sciences, Inc. She initially signed up as a distributor for the company in order to provide vitamin supplements for Sharlie, but soon recognized it as a potential income source. She realized that this was her answer! Collette made it her deliberate intention to become a top-earning distributor for the company so she could support her children and give generously to her favorite charity - the Cystic Fibrosis Foundation. This, of course, was a lofty goal! She rolled up her sleeves and went to work to realize her intention. Within just one year Collette was making in excess of $1,000.00 per week. Her home-based business eventually blossomed into "Larsen Global," a corporation formed and operated by Collette and her two sons. They have one of the most successful distributorships in the network marketing profession. This all began with Collette's decision to create an intention for her life.

Sharlie has also practiced deliberate, *inspired* intention for her own life, amidst numerous difficult challenges related to Cystic Fibrosis. For decades, physicians presented a grim prognosis for Sharlie; at one time she was not expected to live past her 10th birthday. But through the decades, Sharlie has faithfully defied the odds. She has "grown up," married her best friend, and despite fierce discouragement from well-intending physicians, always maintained her dream of being a mother. Collette explains, "It has been Sharlie's intention to be a mom since she received her first Cabbage Patch® doll over 20 years ago." As I interviewed Sharlie, she explained "When people asked me what I wanted to be when I grew up, I always said A MOM. It's all I've ever wanted."

Understanding the risks of pregnancy for someone with Cystic Fibrosis, Sharlie and her husband agreed that they would only proceed once they had each received the inspiration they needed on that matter. After years of prayerful contemplation, that inspiration did come. But the announcement of their pregnancy was quickly met with concerns from medical experts who feared that she would lose her life during delivery. She was advised to terminate the pregnancy. But Sharlie and her husband were faithful to the answer that they'd received and held to their intention to become parents. Sharlie knew that she would be a mother and that she would live to raise her son. Indeed, she has done just that. Their son was 5 years old when Sharlie's heart and lungs finally began to shut down. So, with the support of an entire global community, Sharlie was blessed with what she needed. She endured a risky double-lung and heart transplant. It was no surprise to her countless fans and admirers that she sailed through that grueling and painful surgery almost impeccably.

Today, Sharlie does things that, at one time, she could only dream of. She hikes. She runs. She is one of the most humble people I've ever had the pleasure of knowing. She and her mother, Collette continue to inspire countless people worldwide through keynote speaking, writing, and training. Their unmatched faith in miracles has motivated more people than one could count.

Intention is powerful, particularly when paired with inspiration! These two steps are key ingredients for a successful project, and a successful life!

Practically everyone that I've interviewed for this project has implemented the practice of intention in some form. For some, it was a natural inclination for positivity that made their success inevitable. For others, it was an outlined goal supported by visual reminders, daily affirmations, and organized efforts toward their endeavor. When we combine our deliberate intention with inspiration, we are bound to create a life of purpose and meaning.

Wrapping Up

Intention is a powerful part of this process and a necessary component for any entrepreneur. While inspiration gives us the answers that we need, intention is our active part. Whatever your project is today, create your intention:

- Identify what you want
- Pinpoint your motivation
- Purify your motives
- Declare what you want to achieve
- Cultivate your intention through deliberate thoughts, words, and actions

-

Phase 2 – Building the Project

STEP 3

Build the Mom/Boss Work Schedule

"A vision without a plan is just a dream. A plan without a vision is just drudgery. But a vision with a plan can change the world."
– Old Proverb

There's a good chance that THIS is what you've been waiting for! Phase 2 is entirely devoted to making your project happen! You've strategized your vision. You've developed a noble cause, and you're actively cultivating your intentions for this effort. Now it's time to get organized!

Being an entrepreneur mother takes a special kind of skill. It takes innovation, self-mastery and, of course, ORGANIZATION. Your life has many layers. You have a diverse spectrum of responsibility. But you realize where your number-one priority lies, and frankly, you're not willing to make sacrifices to your family unit for the sake of your project. It's possible to make it all work, but it will take a little preemptive planning. The determining factor in bringing this thing to life while maintaining your family life is your mom/boss schedule - otherwise known as the PRIORITY-BASED schedule. In this chapter, PRIORITY is the bottom line.

In this section, you will assess the important dimensions of your life and then carve out a schedule that satisfies your project, your family needs, and those other important areas. If you're starting to feel uptight at the idea of a schedule, take it from me (a natural-born clutter-case) YOU CAN DO THIS. Once your life is organized in the right way, you'll feel a renewed sense of control and you'll be amazed at what you're able to accomplish in a single day.

Find Meaning in the Monotonous Mandatories

Now, before laying out your new project schedule, it's important to look at everything that's going on in your life. As you lead into this next step, you'll need to account for each area, even the little things! You're going to prevent the "unraveling" before it begins.

If you're typical, "project mode" is defined by a burning drive to get as much done as possible during your waking hours. For many, this means a temporary suspension of normal daily activities. The first activities to go are often the daily monotonous ones. After all, you're in project mode! There are more important things than folding laundry, volunteering in the classroom, driving carpool, and helping with homework. It all seems so... inconsequential?

Here's the thing, as moms, we have countless obligations and responsibilities. Many of those take place within the walls of our homes. Others may take place in the kids' classrooms, in a church responsibility, or even behind the wheel! Every time we devote energy or time to something, we're making a concerted investment in it, a contribution to a greater cause. When something is important, it SHOULD be invested in. But let's face it, some of these "investments" may not be the source of immediate joy. As a mom who has spent many hours driving carpools, I can truly commiserate on how monotonous parenting duties can seem. But the first step in building a mom/boss schedule is recognizing the value of each time contribution in your life, even the monotonous ones - carpool-driving, meal-planning, homework-assisting, nose-wiping, child-bathing, boo-boo-tending, lesson-planning, floor-sweeping, or whatever else makes your home base float. Think about those areas. Give credit to them. Recognize the contribution they are to your family life. We should be careful not to let project demands supersede these important experiences.

Here's a great little exercise that will help you recognize the value of those daily necessities. While seemingly monotonous, the "little things" often have profound significance in the grand scheme of things. They should be your first consideration before devising your mom/boss schedule. For just a moment, consider the following dimensions of your life:

Spiritual

Familial

Marital

Emotional

Social

Physical

Financial

Intellectual

Think of the people and the activities that are associated with each area. How do these dimensions play into your life as a whole? How much of your daily routine contributes to these dimensions? This is something that we don't readily think about. But in reality, our lives are a culmination of multiple roles and responsibilities. We work, we play, we teach, we learn - all of it eventually transpires into the ultimate BIG PICTURE: who we're becoming.

Now, consider which of these areas hold the highest value for you. In the Success Startpack, I've included a diagram for this exercise. Write down these dimensions in order, from most-to-least importance. Then, jot down the activities that are associated with each one. As you view these activities in terms of what they represent, you'll find that many of the perceived "inconsequentials" may actually be of huge consequence. The "little things" are often tied to the dimensions of our lives that MATTER MOST.

As you sketch out your mom/boss schedule, these dimensions will become incredibly relevant. Remember, as we prioritize our lives according to what "matters most," inspiration is most clear. If you want to stay inspired and make the most of this venture, start by building a priority-based schedule. Account for the dimensions of your life that "matter most" BEFORE delving into project demands. You will accomplish more this way!

Identify Your Responsibilities

In order to formulate the best possible schedule for your project, you'll first need to identify the areas of your life that require daily attention. Consider those dimensions of your life that matter most to you. Outline the specific tasks that apply to each dimension. Your family responsibilities might include family date nights, organization of house rules, and time with your family. Within your marriage that will hopefully include date nights, intimate time together, hobbies, and discussions. You may not be able to quantify each experience as a designated "to-do" item, but you should take recognition of the time contribution necessary for each area of your life. Once you have those dimensions accounted for, your project contributions will fit right in!

Start by making a list that includes each role in your life: Mother, wife, entrepreneur, sister, friend… List each of them! Next, jot down the daily "necessities" associated with each of these roles. If your family relies on you to get dinner made, include it. If you drive kids to school, include that. If you have a spouse, include the contributions that are associated with that role as well. A chart is provided for you in the Success Startpack to help you get these roles and responsibilities laid out!

Write a Priority-Based Schedule

Now, it's time to formulate your new mom/boss schedule. In this process, you're going to account for each moment of your day. Don't worry, you'll still have some down time. That will be scheduled in as well. As mentioned, by accounting for each moment, you'll naturally contribute more of yourself, knowing that you've allotted that time for a certain special purpose. Family time, drive time, meal time, and project time will consequently be more productive and more meaningful.

A schedule template sheet is ready for you in the Success Startpack to help get your new mom/boss schedule started! Here's a sample to get you thinking (My 2014 Work Schedule)

	Mon	Tues	Wed	Thur	Fri
6am	Exercise Scripture Prayer	Exercise Scripture Prayer	Exercise Scripture Prayer	Exercise Scripture Prayer	Exercise Scripture Prayer
7am	Ready For School	Ready For School	Ready For School	Ready For School	Ready For School
8am	Carpool	Carpool	Carpool	Carpool	Carpool
9-12	Gavin & Mom	Gavin & Mom	Gavin & Mom	Gavin & Mom	Gavin & Mom
12-3	**WORK**	**WORK**	**WORK**	**WORK**	**WORK**
3pm	Carpool	Carpool	Carpool	Carpool	Carpool
4pm	Homework	Homework	Homework	Homework	Friends
5pm	Dinner Family Time	Dinner Family Time	Dinner Family Time	Dinner Family Time	Pizza & Date Night
6pm	Power Hour	Power Hour	Power Hour	Power Hour	Date Night
7pm	FAMILY NIGHT	Down Time	Down Time	Down Time	Date Night
8pm	Prayer Story Bedtime	Prayer Story Bedtime	Prayer Story Bedtime	Prayer Story Bedtime	Prayer Story Bedtime
9pm	Elective	Elective	Elective	Elective	Elective
10pm	Elective	Elective	Elective	Elective	Elective
10:30	Sleep	Sleep	Sleep	Sleep	Sleep

Here are a few things about my schedule that are worth noting:

- Two hours of elective time is left every evening. That's a variable time expenditure that depends on kids' after-school activities, extra carpool runs, or other obligations. When left open, that time can be spent doing some extra work, helping kids with projects/homework, house cleaning, or having one-on-one time with the kids. I tailor those blocks based on what's needed that day. Very often, after-school "waiting" time (orthodontics appointments, practices, or lessons) can be easily filled with a running list of project responsibilities or personal down time. You will need elective time as well. Schedule it in.

- The "Gavin and Mom" time in the morning is often when I arrange playdates, one-on-one time, or morning errands. Anything that I have going in the morning happens with that little buddy in mind. The hours that are spent with Gavin are special because he's still young. One day soon, I won't have as much individual time with him during the day. Therefore, I try to make that time special. Although we may be running errands together, I try to stay off of my phone. The same goes for any other time with the kids or husband. Stay off of the phone. Make the time special, regardless of what you're doing.

- Friday nights are left open for my husband and me. That's one important contribution to our relationship. We decided a long time ago that date night was a MUST so we always leave that time open just for the two of us.

- Although this schedule may look painfully rigid, there's always room for adjustments. You might notice that there is no schedule on Saturday or Sunday. Those days are left open for family time, parties, chores, camping trips, church meetings, and down time. Our family does an hour of hard, fast work on Saturday morning, but aside from that (and church meetings on Sunday), we keep weekends low key!

Separate and Maximize Your Daily Responsibilities

As I interviewed various moms about their "project time," I wanted to pinpoint their secrets for making it all work. This idea of separating and maximizing our responsibilities seems pretty consistent among the women that I spoke with. I love this concept. When it comes to creating "balance," I believe that this is the key.

When you're first starting a project, it's tempting to allow that project time to absorb all of you. But it's important that we don't let this happen. Your family needs you to be present for them. But the reality is, when you own a business, your project needs you as well. This technique is basically a shift in mindset. It begins when we view each of those daily routines as a separate, meaningful contribution that requires our individual attention. Whether it's date night, bathing a child, driving kids to school, or working on the project, know that each experience is an investment in something bigger. We must be present in these important moments as they're happening. Rather than allowing emails, phone calls, or social media time to bleed into precious family time, preschedule your email, phone calls, and media posts. When we're on a date night, we should really BE on a date night. When we're at a park day with the kids; we should be at park day. And of course, when it's time to work, we should really work.

As you lay out your daily responsibilities, consider how you can maximize each one. When driving alone in the car, I often use that time to listen to audiobooks or podcasts. When my kids are there with me, I try to make the most of that time with them too. We might prep for quizzes, discuss school happenings, rock out to music, or just talk. There are ways that you can make EVEN CARPOOL driving more meaningful. Once you have your day on paper, you'll see where you can best-maximize your moments, even those mandatory monotonous ones.

I don't mean to suggest that we should be exhaustedly busy all of the time. In fact, with this approach, you can actually move from a state of overwhelm into a place of fulfillment. From what I've experienced, overwhelm comes when I'm zeroed in on too much of the same thing. When we lack balance it's like paddling on one side of the boat over and over again. We find ourselves going in circles, never actually getting anywhere.

With this approach, you're not lackadaisically floating from one unplanned moment to another OR allowing project demands to override other important aspects of your life. You will find that as you develop a more organized day and learn to devote yourself fully to each individual experience, you will be more fulfilled in your role as a mother and more accomplished in your project.

Carve Out an "Isolated Work Block"

An "isolated work block" is a predesignated block of time during the day to devote yourself solely to your project and nothing else. While this concept may seem counterintuitive to your desire for a balanced home life, it is absolutely in the best interest of your family to arrange your mom/boss schedule this way! Through this approach, you'll pre-arrange your work time and delve into the project ONLY during that time. Then, when your work block is over, you're available for the other responsibilities in your life!

Depending on where you are in life, your work block may be during nap time, during a child swap, or while the kids are at school. It will be as long as you decide it to be, based on what you're able and willing to do. You may need to approach the project in phases, knowing that you'll have more time during the day as your kids get older. You may also consider whether it's worth arranging a few hours of child care each week. Consider where you are in life and strategize at least one or two isolated work blocks each week.

This approach is an alternative to the typical (but largely unsuccessful) routine of juggling kids as you work. Let's face it, collaborating kids and work responsibilities hardly ever pans out. We all know why; the kids get ignored while the project takes precedence. Work/Family boundaries become blurry. This is not an ideal way to run a business, or a home! With that approach, you'll begin to feel guilty about losing precious time with your kids, your family will become frustrated as responsibilities come unraveled, and "the project" will eventually become a source of stress. Start from the beginning by arranging an isolated work block!

When I interviewed renowned Chef and business owner/mompreneur, Kari Rich, she explained that two hours of planned and focused project time is always more productive than working intermittently throughout the day. Kari often relies on a two-hour work block while her young daughter is with a sitter. During those two hours, she devotes herself FULLY to her project, squeezing in as much work as possible. Then, during non-working hours, she can place project responsibilities aside and devote herself entirely to her family. This is a routine that many mompreneurs rely on! Most of the women that I've interviewed schedule babysitting for non-school age kids for just 2-3 hours, a few days per week in order to get their project work done. Others will swap babysitting with a friend. During that uninterrupted time, they PLOW through their work load! This approach carries over into their parenting experience, allowing them to devote all of themselves in each moment for whatever it represents.

Get Rid of the Unnecessary Stuff

As you etch out your schedule, be sure to limit social media, television, and pointless time-expenditures. You'll likely find that in doing so, you'll have plenty of time to improve on the dimensions of your life that matter most and build your project!

If you're invested in your project vision, you'll be willing to make sacrifices where they're necessary. It won't be in your family time. It will be from somewhere else. Hobbies may have to be put on hold. Friend time may also go to the backburner. Decide what's necessary and be a wise steward over the time that you've been gifted. This approach will make all the difference in your ability to build your project while preserving your family unit.

Revamp Household Assignments

As you add your project responsibilities to your already-busy daily routine, there will most likely be a shuffle in other areas. To buffer this "domino effect," it's helpful to revamp household assignments, spreading out those mandatory chores to all of the members of the household. First consider: are you taking on responsibilities that should otherwise be done by one of the kids? How about laundry? Are you doing laundry for a kid that could do it himself? What about dishes or sweeping floors? A reorganization of household tasks can make all the difference in the running of your household. Assess the situation, take your family size and the age of your kids into consideration and allow each family member to participate where possible. This will not only decrease your task list, it will produce more-productive, responsible, and confident kids! Check TheSuccessProject.com for my favorite "chore" programs and resources.

Eliminate Distractions

Telling a mommy to eliminate distractions might be like telling a fish to stay away from water. Distractions are basically the name of the game when you're a mom, but there are certain disruptions that are avoidable. You can make the best of your work time, family time, and every other time by setting a few ground rules for yourself.

As mentioned, the time that you have allocated for the project should ONLY include action items for the project itself. Spending two uninterrupted hours on your project will produce a bigger contribution than spending eight hours of unfocused time bouncing between projects. Since your project will likely involve being on the computer, you should consider shutting down those probable interruptions: Pinterest, Facebook, or even email.

My allotted period of time for this book project was 3 hours, 4 days per week, from 12-3pm. It doesn't sound like much, does it? The reality is that I'm a mom and a wife in addition to countless other roles in my life. I don't have 12 hours a day to work so I must make those minutes count. I turn off the text on my phone to avoid distractions and do my best to follow my action item list.

During many of the interviews conducted for this project, the subject of "scheduling" came up. When I posed the topic to award-winning book author and mother-of-twins, Heidi Andrews, she responded with these great insights:

- Always have a priority list and limit the list. When you keep the priority list short, you're more likely to get those most-important items done.
- Put the phone away. Pick it up 2-3 times a day to check email. Picking it up frequently will chop up family time.

- Have a regular routine to manage your time and your sanity
- Have a weekly meeting to keep things in check
- Get work done during nap times and other "down time"

Making the Mom/Boss Schedule Really Work

- Take all aspects of your schedule seriously. If you don't, no one else will.
- Consider where you are in life to determine how much you can take on. (kids' nap times, school hours, bedtime...)
- Before committing to your new work schedule, it's best to consult your partner in crime. Decide (together) if the schedule seems reasonable. As you begin your project, you'll feel better about your work endeavors if they're supported by your spouse.
- Take reflective time seriously. Even if it's for five minutes, take time each morning to pray for guidance, set your plan, and visualize goals. You will accomplish more everywhere if you do this.

Wrapping Up

The first stage of planning for your new project is schedule organization. Take all aspects of your life into consideration when devising your work schedule. Consider what projects are appropriate for your stage in life. Map out a maximum MOM/BOSS schedule by accounting for each area of responsibility in your life.

Take your schedule seriously and don't get distracted. Shut down any probable distractions as you sit down to work. Be mindful of the time that you have allocated for each respective purpose. Kid time, date nights, carpool, cooking, working. Each experience has specific demands. Fulfill your purpose in each area of your life by compartmentalizing each area of your schedule. Don't allow your work to bleed over into your family time. Though it is tempting as you embark on your new plans, be mindful of this time in your life. The kids are still young and you won't have this experience again.

STEP 4

Do Your Research

"Research is what I'm doing when I don't know what I'm doing."
- Wernher Von Braun

Now that you've carved out your designated work time, you might be tempted to start delving into project development! But if you really want a viable project, you must follow due diligence, that includes research! There is just no excuse for skipping research. It is SO EASY and the resources that you need are likely sitting in front of you! Research will be your key to producing a solid vision and a solid game plan. Before you begin project development, see what's working for other companies. And just as well, find out what isn't working! What processes should be implemented? What are your marketing requirements? Your time is precious and should be spent the right way. Research will help you find the correct path!

Start by answering some basic questions about your project. Making a general assessment of your plan will help you create a roadmap and hopefully eliminate any potential roadblocks along the way.

Clearly define the following:
- What product/service am I offering?
- Who will want to buy my service/product?
- What tools and resources should I implement?
- How will I sell and/or advertise my service/product?
- What are other businesses like mine doing to be successful?

The first phase of project development should be spent answering these questions! Research will be the key to developing a solid plan.

Don't Reinvent the Wheel

During your research process, you will inevitably discover the tools and resources that ALREADY exist. You don't need to start from scratch for most anything that you pursue because people have likely already paved the path for you. This is true for almost any new innovation. Even the most revolutionary technologies didn't spring from nothing. Practically every new innovation is birthed through a series of predecessors, each making a key improvement that eventually forms the final product. You're likely not going to create something that no one's ever heard of. MAYBE, but not likely. Some of the best new things have been merely an improvement on something that's already out there. As you research ideas, see what resonates with you. Don't try to compete with what's there, build on it! Make it yours.

Through research, you can also find the tools you'll need to make your project a success. Find out what others like you are doing! What systems make book-keeping easier? What PR approaches are most-successful? Draw on your own innovations as well as the strengths of others in order to formulate a good game plan. If you do the research, you'll find that much of what you need is already there.

When my step mom, Dr. Gaila Mackenzie-Strawn was in the process of expanding her private health practice, she realized that the office was in need of some serious protocol updates. Her *pen and paper* scheduling system made it difficult for patients to make appointments. She began by researching other physician websites and found that most private practices similar to hers offered an online scheduling system. After a weekend of research, she integrated a scheduling system to her website. Within just a few months, her revenue QUADRUPLED!

Do your research and gather ideas that are proven! And for heaven's sake, don't waste time REINVENTING THE WHEEL!

Consult an Expert

In the midst of your new project, you may find that some requirements lie within your "NO CLUE" zone. Don't let that be a deal-breaker! You're not going to be an expert at everything. Just know that there are some things you have to learn. You might not have the capital necessary to outsource everything in your "NO CLUE" zone. Resources are everywhere: books, classes, web tutorials, the list goes on! An excellent option is a consultation with someone who knows what they're doing.

When I owned a small theater school, I needed help with marketing but could not afford to bring on a full-time marketing specialist. Besides, I wanted to do the marketing myself. As a solution, I scheduled a phone consultation with one of San Diego's premier marketing specialists for dance studios. I purchased a one-hour consultation for $100. In that time, I asked every feasible question regarding advertising, print marketing, and networking. She gave me a wealth of knowledge! During that one-hour phone call, I learned specifically how to advertise in local elementary schools, my options as a nonprofit, and how to create an overall draw to the community through concepts that had never-before occurred to me! That phone call set the foundation for my marketing model for that business - and all for $100!

I repeated this process several times, also consulting with a business owner in Virginia (who actually spoke to me for free). She gave me the pros and cons regarding the process of working as a nonprofit and gave me a great deal of seasoned guidance for my project. That experience taught me that people are often happy to impart their wisdom and experience! If you decide to take this approach, be humble about it. Start by conveying a respect for their business, then pose a no-pressure request for their time. Once you get something scheduled, have your questions ready! While not everyone will respond to your request, there are many successful professionals who are willing to help a new entrepreneur.

As Jennifer Sattley started her amazingly successful food blog, Carlsbad Cravings, she contacted her favorite food bloggers for advice. She asked the women for their "3 best tips" for starting and running a food blog. Jennifer received several valuable insights that have proven to be key factors in the success of her business. They came through her simple willingness to reach out and ask for help!

Web Research

Much of your research has likely already taken place over the internet. And that's an excellent place to start. You may not need to go any further than your home computer. You can learn quite a lot about most companies by studying their website and their social media pages, particularly for a clue-in to product sales and marketing.

For other aspects of the business, software tools, outsourcing options, product development resources, Q &

A sites are also a great option. You can get a wide spectrum of insights for practically anything through question/answer forums. Search for companies like yours. Join discussion groups. Be generous with what you've learned and get additional knowledge from others.

Wrapping Up

- Find out what's out there. Seek out the tips and tools to make your project smooth, efficient, and up-to-date! Realize that you don't have to reinvent the wheel. Generally, it's best to build on the innovations of others rather than building from scratch.
- Be willing to speak to people that know more than you do. Consult with the experts.
- Use the internet to study other business models, search forums, and gain knowledge from others

STEP 5

Translate Your Vision into an Action Plan

"A goal without a plan is just a wish."
-Antion e de Saint-Exupery

Once you've made the decision to pursue a particular intention and you're committed to receiving and acting on inspiration, you will be astounded at how clearly and abundantly you're flooded with ideas. If you're not prepared sufficiently to capture this detailed plan, it will go floating into the wind. Step 5 is all about capturing and organizing those inspired ideas. The beginning may feel a little sticky or discombobulated, but I assure you, once you begin organizing those details, you'll experience a free-flow of insights! Remember, you are the vehicle to this inspired endeavor. If you manage it wisely, you'll be given all you need to make it happen!

The Idea Throw-down

When starting a new business, how do you possibly know where to start? For most projects, the process will include multiple tasks such as building a blog or a website, making networking connections, drawing up a marketing strategy, production planning and so forth. But how do you know WHERE to start? What comes first? If you don't want to waste time, you'll need to get all of those steps laid out and organized in a start-to-finish format.

Begin by throwing all of your ideas down on paper! These ideas can be broad or specific. From website color schemes, to print ideas, to campaign concepts - if it's something that you can think of, write it down. Draw on your research during this process. If you've found marketing tools that appeal to you, include those. Print out pictures if you like. You will not have all of the details from the start, that's completely normal. At this point, just write down anything that you can think of. Up until this point, this has likely just been an idea. This process puts your idea into motion. Whatever is inside your head, WRITE IT DOWN.

Once you've thrown down all of the components that you can see, evaluate and prioritize them. If "build a website" is one of your top items then you'll need to "throw down" all of the prerequisite steps that are necessary to make that happen. You can't begin building your site until you have a domain name and a content management system. At some point, you'll also need images, a template, social media, and so forth. This single component can seem overwhelming until you chunk it down into its separate, achievable steps.

Finally, evaluate and organize all of your pieces until the entire project is laid out from start to finish. There may be twenty steps. There may be a hundred steps. Lay them all out until you can see your starting point and your finish line. As you delve in, you will likely reorganize, add items, subtract items, the point is, you now have an idea of what's necessary and where to start.

The Project Planner

I'm passionate about this concept and have created dozens of project planners through the years. For a mom that doesn't have ten hours a day to work, this portable option makes keeping ideas simple. I use this concept to organize not only the framework for my business ventures, but also personal goal plans and events that I'm coordinating. The idea here is to take the components from your idea "throw-down" and expand on them with every necessary detail. This planner will become your reference guide each time you sit down to work, and you'll always have a place to file away new ideas. The project planner should cover the details of this project from start to finish. *A formatted Project Planner is available at my website,*

TheSuccessProject.com for purchase, or you can use a lined journal of your choice!

Here's how to organize your planner:

Vision Statement

Every project should begin with a vision statement. Write yours in the front of your planner. This is your intention for the project, the future and ultimate goal of the business! In some cases, a vision statement can be summed up in a few words or a few sentences. This statement may include specific goals that represent the inherent nature of the business, the impact it will have in the world, the company's commitment to the customer, and so forth. You might also want to reflect your motive for this project within your vision statement. Analyze your primary goals and vision for this project and reflect them in your vision statement. Try not to make it too detailed, or too brief.

As you develop your vision statement, think beyond the basic functions of your business, and identify your secret sauce... the thing that makes your project special. What are you offering that sets you apart from the rest? This point will be beneficial in bringing others aboard and it will narrow your purpose, helping you identify the necessary components of your project plan.

Here is my vision statement for The Success Project: 10 Steps for the Mompreneur: *To inspire and encourage home-*

based moms in their entrepreneurial ambitions while helping them preserve the dimensions of life that matter most.

Project Elements

The next step in the project-building phase is to organize the pieces that you've brainstormed. Again, this is my approach, whimsical as it may seem, I totally recommend it. It is a great way to take a ton of ideas and streamline them into an organized format.

At the front of your journal, create a list of project elements. Each project element serves as a chapter heading for your planner. List each one in a table of contents at the front of your book. Here's a sample:

	Project Element
1	Research Write Business Plan
2	Write an ebook
3	Develop corresponding web tutorial script
4	Expand web tutorial into Powerpoint presentation
5	Obtain domain name for project
6	Develop Website
7	Shoot Video Segments
8	Integrate video
9	Integrate membership component
10	Establish email campaign resources
11	Establish social media channels
12	Integrate social media marketing and campaigns

Once your Table of Contents is complete, thumb through your book and every several pages, insert a new chapter heading. Those empty pages will soon be filled with the details for each project element. This is where you'll incorporate all of those details from your project list plus any new details that you come upon. Here you will organize them, and possibly give each item a timetable for completion. This will become your reference guide for this project; a portable file cabinet of sorts. My own project planners are filled with hand-written lists, names, email addresses, websites, online courses, images, flow charts, written diagrams, and everything else related to the project at hand. This is where all of the project vision and detail is stored! As time goes on, the pages of your planner will fill up.

As you find answers, journal them in your planner! Keep your planner with you so that that you can jot down new ideas as they come. This is particularly helpful in the beginning phases of development. When you start looking for inspiration, you will find it in places that you least expect! If you come across a great detail that you need, record it under the corresponding chapter heading. Side note: Many of my best inspirations happen as I'm falling asleep at night. For this reason, my project planner sleeps on the night stand next to me!

This is extremely useful, particularly as you encounter resources for future portions of your plan. Let's say, for instance, that while I'm developing my E-book (chapter 2) I meet a college student that's looking for an internship opportunity in video production. While I'm not yet ready to start video for my project, I'm able to file this resource, knowing that in the future I'll need a videographer. I jot down his name and contact information under my "video" section, and let him know that I'll be contacting him in 4-5 weeks, according to my schedule. Although you won't see all of the details from the start, this information organization process will certainly get your game plan started.

Wrapping Up

Start with your idea "throw down." List essential items and information gathered through your research. Customize a project planner that will serve as a place to organize those big ideas. Organize your planner with chapter headings, each representing the key components to your project. Refer to it as your own instruction manual and a source for your action item list. As you come upon more ideas and project details, file them in your project planner.

STEP 6

Manage Your Project

"If you are clear about your goals and take several steps in the right direction every day, eventually you will succeed. So decide what it is you want, write it down, review it constantly, and each day do something that moves you toward those goals."
-Jack Canfield

While it may seem like overkill to formally manage a project that you're flying solo on, studies have consistently proven that good management is the difference between a project that flies and one that falls flat. Statistics prove that entrepreneurs who set measurable goals and track project details are consistently more successful. If you want your *great idea* to see the light of day, you'll need to strategize a goal plan, institute a project timeline, know when to outsource, and maintain regular checkpoints. These are skills that anyone can learn. Here's how to get started:

Establish Measurable Goals

Every business starts with a goal; it's the one thing that we all have in common. And while the basic goal of every business is obvious (of course, to grow the business) we should be much more specific about what we want to achieve. In fact, it's important to develop and implement goals for each aspect of the project. This is the key to growing a successful business.

Project goals should be specific and measurable. In other words, a goal should be something that you can accomplish every day or every week – something that can be accounted for with a checkmark. "Become a top-grossing sales representative" is a great vision, but it's not a great goal. Begin with whatever that vision is and create smaller, achievable steps that will lead you to that final outcome. Here's an example of a measurable goal that would support the vision of "becoming a top-grossing sales representative:"

   ✓ *Reach out to 50 companies each day for the next 30 days and offer an introductory service or free product.*

Now, that's a goal that can be accomplished! It's a small step that leads to the greater vision. You might have a vision to create better communication with your customer. Again, it's a nice vision, but not a measurable goal. Start with the vision and develop action steps that will contribute to that cause:

✓ *Implement a birthday card mailer*

✓ *Ask a question on social media once a week that engages your followers*

Those are both goals that can be planned on a calendar, check-marked, and tracked.

Start developing goals by separating the project into parts, for instance: product development, marketing, merchandizing, sales, content development, social media marketing, email outreach, networking – or whatever else applies to your project. Then, consider appropriate goals to apply within each area. Remember, these are things that you can measure and account for.

Action Items

Whether you're completing the work yourself or hiring out, it's helpful to approach your work block with an itemized list of action items. I generally pull goals from my project planner and compile a list that will satisfy an entire portion of the project. For instance, I might have an entire list devoted to content development for a website.

Each day, I'm able to checkmark action items as they're completed. Day after day, I begin my work wherever I left off on the previous day. There's no strategizing, it's all laid out for me each day.

You might consider designating a specific day each week to a certain portion of your project. Mondays for content writing, Tuesdays for email outreach, Wednesdays for social media and so forth. Each project component will have its own action item list.

Create a Timeline and Manage with Checkpoints

Take the time to periodically check in to verify that your project is coming through on the time frame that you've outlined. It may be necessary to redefine your expectations, change gears, or allow more time where necessary. The point is that you're maintaining accountability for yourself. It might sound silly to set deadlines for yourself. But in order to make progress and to ensure that your project timeline is conducive to your family time, you must pay attention to that timeline. Check in once in a while to make sure that goals are being met at their designated timeframe, and reevaluate when modifications are necessary.

Know When to Outsource

There are high demands for any new entrepreneur. In the beginning, you will likely be in charge of every aspect of your business; branding, financials, distribution, marketing, information, publishing, technology, and so forth! But good project management often includes outsourcing. When the demands of a particular process disable you from achieving the high-level management necessary for your project's survival, send the job to someone else. In this day in age, it's possible to outsource practically every aspect of your business. Before you decide WHAT to outsource, consider your primary role in the business. That's what you should spend your time and energy doing. When necessary tasks will take you away from your primary function, outsource them.

For one of my business projects, I need a custom badge made each new year for our partners to display on their websites. I can either spend several hours on Photoshop, mocking up a subpar graphic badge OR I can outsource that portion of the project to a graphic designer for under $10. It's true. Through online outsourcing companies, you can literally purchase graphic work, marketing gigs, print design, and templates for practically nothing. These companies offer a long line of independent contractors that are ready to complete a custom job at high speed and high quality!

As you form your business model, determine what aspects of the business you should have your hands in. If graphic design is something you need, but it's not an integral part of the business, (or something that you're trained in) that may be a good aspect to outsource. On the other hand, if you run a blog that is specific to you and your expertise, then article-writing is probably something you should always do yourself. Understand where your priorities are within the business and determine where your time should be spent. There are contractors available within practically every industry. Determine your needs, your personal priorities, and outsource where possible. This can make all the difference in the success of your project! Check my website, TheSuccessProject.com for updates on my favorite companies to work with.

Schedule Additional Research

When you hit a road bump, don't be afraid to schedule additional research. Scheduling your research is a more-effective approach than thumbing through your phone throughout your work periods. You will find that one hour of deliberate research time will go further than two discombobulated hours of researching, writing, and checking your email. Also consider adding it to your action item list at the beginning of each new phase and use this time to dig out details. Study business models of companies similar to yours. Participate in social media groups and subscribe to email campaigns. Find out how it all works and decide what practices you'll adopt! A little bit of planning will go a long way!

The Secret to Working at Lightning Speed

Here's the secret: PLAN AHEAD. I learned this concept when I was running the theater company. It just so happened that I was also called to serve as the president of the young women's organization at my church at that time as well. It was a crazy time in my life. Joyful, but busy. The only way to survive those two projects at the same time was to plan ahead. Not just weeks or days ahead – I needed to plan the entire year in advance! I would sit down with a calendar and account for every activity, every play, camp, class, and facility reservation. At the beginning of the year I knew when my audition days would fall, when my camps would be, and when to order music, advertise for shows, book theater spaces, and so forth. This kind of planning saves hours of time. You never have to think about what you're going to do each day. It's all laid out for you. Literally ONE DAY of planning will make the rest of the year a breeze.

Plan your project in advance. Choose campaigns ahead of time and map out your Instagram posts, your videos, your interviews, your sales, giveaways, and whatever else relates to your business! If you know ahead of time that you want to collaborate, get those names and ideas down on paper and you'll be more inclined to reach out during your designated period of time. Consider mapping out a product photography day, an email writing day (possibly for several weeks of emails), a content writing day, an outreach day, and so on. As you accumulate resources for the future, you will become incredibly efficient during that work hour. Your photos for Instagram will be ready, your interviews will be booked, your email campaigns will be written, and here's a bonus: whatever aspects of this process are intimidating to you have now been reduced to an item waiting for a checkmark. So go ahead and plan all of those BIG MOVES. You're making your dreams a reality.

Use Multiple Approaches

As you delve into management and marketing, it's a good idea to experiment with multiple strategies, particularly in the beginning. There are countless potential approaches. Don't get stuck inside the box! Try something you haven't tried before: Identify important contacts and send them a note with a free product, host an event, offer to guest blog on someone's site or offer yourself as a guest interview on a podcast.

Research different ways to get your product "out there" and try them out! If you're consistently employing different strategies, you'll cover more ground and inevitably get the word out to more potential customers.

The Inevitable Trial Phase

During the initial phases of your project, keep in mind that there may be a period of trial and error. Don't be afraid to try new things. Take surveys. Implement tools that are used by other businesses like yours. You may hit it the first time or you may experience a learning curve. Trial and error is not the end. In fact, it's very often the means to providing the correct answers. Modify your action plan where necessary! Don't hesitate to go back to the drawing board.

Wrapping Up

Successful Project management includes the following:

- Setting daily measureable goals for your project
- Managing your project with periodic check points
- Outsourcing where necessary
- Continuing research through the duration of your project
- Employing multiple approaches throughout the process.

Phase 3 – Amazing Fabulous You

STEP 7

Be the Ultimate Time Manager

"All we have to decide is what to do with the time that is given us."
-J.R.R. Tolkien

The thing that differentiates this book from others written about entrepreneurship is the *Mommy* factor. Remember, this isn't JUST about project planning. It's about how to make it ALL WORK: every aspect of your life, including the project. If there's one thing that you should remember in the scope of many things we've discussed it's this: The way that we spend our time is everything.

It's no mistake that I've placed this step on time management directly after project management. See, as you delve into these exciting aspects of your project, time will slip by. You could feasibly spend hours upon hours delving into this aspect of your new business as the minutes of your "family time" also slip by. Don't make that mistake. Remember that time is precious and you'll need to make the most of it – for your project AND your family. Let's take a few minutes to reflect on this pivotal resource!

For starters, have you ever taken a moment to consider how much of your life is comprised of sleeping, eating, texting, talking, working, playing, and every other activity that contributes to your day? Over a lifetime, most humans spend twenty-six years sleeping. If you're typical, you can spend a year of your lifetime fixing your hair, nine years watching television, and as much as ten years of your life on social media. Amazing, isn't it?

The way that you divide your day is the way you divide your life. Most of us underestimate the contribution of those small routines. But everything adds up! The decision to set aside even one hour per week for a specific purpose can influence the course of your life. Family nights, dinners, reading sources, television material, meaningful conversations, working out, and hours working – it all adds up and contributes to the final outcome, YOUR LIFE! While big decisions can certainly change the course of our lives, it is the small daily decisions that determine our destination.

As plans for your project begin to take shape, recognize your time as a resource, one for which you have a stewardship OVER. You decide how you'll spend that time. You decide how you give it to others. Take accountability for where that precious time is going. Even 5 minutes a day will go a long way!

One of my favorite success stories is again from Olympic athlete, Peter Vidmar - Back to that youth conference that I attended in San Diego! In addition to discussing his visualization exercises to prepare for the Olympics, Vidmar also described his action plan! He and a fellow gymnast made the decision to spend an extra fifteen minutes training each night after the rest of the athletes retired for bed. He explained that upon calculating 15 minutes per day over the course of a year, they discovered that this plan would result in 91 extra training hours in a year. When you're talking about the OLYMPICS, you can imagine that it's worth every minute of training. Peter Vidmar won 3 Olympic medals that year including two golds and one silver. He attributes his success, in part, to that extra time spent training in the gym, fifteen extra minutes each day.

This story prompted quite an epiphany for me. It made me realize how much each moment of our day counts. And although you probably aren't training for the Olympics, THIS is the performance of your life! So HOW are you spending the hours and minutes of your day? Are you creating your legacy? Are you creating the life that you want? Minutes turn into hours, hours into days, and days eventually turn into months and years of your life. Spend your minutes wisely – make them count! Every mother should realize that TIME is the greatest resource that we have. The way that we use it is EVERYTHING.

Here are a few ways to completely change the way that you utilize your time.

Give Up a Habit

In a speech that I attended years ago, I was issued a challenge to give up a single habit that was holding me back. I'd actually heard the challenge before but on this particular occasion, I was compelled to answer the call. I recognized that even a small habit, when eliminated permanently, could change the course of my life. I thought of numerous things that I could live without, but one certainly seemed most pressing. At the time, I had become somewhat addicted to a particular television network. As new shows were added, my repertoire of shows increased. Before I knew it, I was watching TV for two hours EVERY night after the kids went to bed. I realized that this was the habit that I needed to kick. Not because I thought that television was inherently bad, I just felt inspired to remove this habit from my life. It wasn't easy and I had a little withdrawal in the beginning. But with the elimination of that television time, my mind became clearer and more focused. Within 10 months of removing that habit, I had the inspiration to write THIS BOOK!

Giving up a time-consuming habit can literally change the course of your life. No exaggeration! But small habits make a difference as well. Think about what you have going on and determine whether you can give something up. It might affect the way that you see the world. It may open those windows of inspiration, and perhaps it will be the determining factor for your project altogether! Consider where you're spending your time and give up a habit that's holding you back!

Add a Habit

Years ago, I learned of a man who was serving in an unpaid clergy position for his church while running a particularly time-intensive project at work. He was also the father to a growing family. In an effort to maintain his priorities as a father during this chaotic time in his life, he decided to establish a few new habits that would contribute to the things that mattered most to him: his wife and children. His first decision was to ALWAYS make it to the kids' big stuff: games, recitals, shows, and presentations. He would make a habit of it! Although he wouldn't make it to many practices or pastimes, he would not let anything get in the way of those big events, regardless of anything else going on in his busy life! Secondly, he began a routine of talking with his kids one-on-one. He describes these meet-ups often sitting in the kid's room, sometimes both of them laying on the bed staring at the ceiling as they talked about life. Although the man's life was still very busy, those chosen moments transpired into some of the most important contributions to their family over the course of those years.

As you evaluate your life, consider what additional habit would benefit your family. Start a tradition of doing something each day, each week, or maybe each month. Reading a book to your kids, having a conversation, making a date night... whatever it is, make it a habit! Again, this small decision may completely change the outcome of your life.

The Power Hour

This chapter on time management would not be complete without the concept of the POWER HOUR! First of all, this is a clever name, but in reality, it doesn't have to last an hour. It can be two hours, twenty minutes, or sixty seconds! To illustrate what a POWER HOUR is, just think back on the last time unexpected guests called to announce that they were five from your house. We've all been there. Best-case scenario, you get a phone call - worst-case, just a knock at the door. This company suddenly becomes the source of your most-productive five minutes of the week. Am I right? During that time, you get couch cushions back in place, toys picked up off of the floor, dishes away, counters wiped, and MAYBE even the toilets scrubbed out. Although it's not a thorough cleaning job, you know from experience JUST how much is possible in 5 minutes!

Just think of how much you'd get done if you allotted one entire power hour every day. That time might be used to wipe counters, put away toys, organize a book shelf, fold laundry, or make your bed. In fact, you'd likely get all of that done in one session. This habit should make a nice addition to your daily routine now that you've devoted more of your time to your project. The idea is to move quickly, getting a LOT done in a short window of time. I find myself squeezing in a "power-20" right after school drop-off. In 20 minutes, you can get breakfast dishes cleaned up, counters wiped down, and floors swept.

We've extended this concept to our entire family with a "5-Minute Cleanup" routine just before bedtime. It's the kids' time to run around the house, pick up their messes and put away shoes and backpacks, all within 5 minutes. It's a speed fest of cleaning and tidying and a definite success secret for the do-it-all mom!

Multitasking – the good, the bad, and the ugly

Over the span of time, mothers have rightfully earned recognition for being the world's best multitaskers. Everyone knows it. Just think of the morning routine... scrambling eggs while running a spelling quiz and simultaneously reminding the other kid to pack his lunch. Sound familiar? Of course! This is part of your job description. Do things quickly, and simultaneously! But let's be honest. The dynamics of multitasking in the modern, digital age have morphed into something else, altogether. Now that social media, email, and texting seem to be an hourly obligation, we find ourselves committing to these tasks amidst the more meaningful experiences of our lives. Kids' bedtimes, morning drives to school, dinners, park days, reading time - how many of these organic life experiences (that probably fall into your "matters most" category) are now subject to such important tasks as checking your email, updating Instagram, or checking Facebook.

Here's the thing. Multitasking is part of your life. You're probably really good at it. But you have to decide where your boundaries are. Make a concerted effort to multitask the right way, rather than letting those moment-to-moment "demands" determine where your attention goes.

Here's a simple qualifier when determining whether you're willing to split the task. Ask yourself whether it's an organic life experience. Let me explain: An organic life experience is something that involves you and other humans as you are in the simplest, purist form. Organic life experiences are the things we do without any requirement for modern digital device: gardening, swimming, having a meaningful conversation, sitting on the beach, cooking a meal, putting kids to bed, reading, or just *thinking*. These organic experiences become the fabric of our lives. They're what memories are made of and they contribute to *who we are*. These organic experiences tend to blend really well together. For the most part, it's possible to multitask organic experiences in meaningful ways - maintaining your focus, and staying in tuned. Want to spend time with a kid? Have that child sit at the counter and talk while you make dinner! There you have two important contributions to your life, happening at once. Better yet, teach her how to cook! Plan a service project together. Scramble the eggs while running that spelling quiz! Consider areas of your life that matter most and streamline those activities into your life's daily obligations.

Any experience that centers on a digital interface is NOT an organic life experience. I don't mean to condemn modern technology. All of my projects involve technology, almost solitarily. But you must be careful. Don't combine your digital obligations with your human interaction. Being a parent requires you to be present and you are simply NOT present when you update your status, check your email, or text a friend. When you're with your kids or your friends, put your phone away. Focus on what's in front of you and devote your energy to that one thing. Let your email and social media take place during a specifically designated portion of your day and you'll be more effective in those efforts as well. Remember, each moment serves as a contribution to something. Decide what each moment represents and let that be your focus.

Start With What Matters

The beautiful thing about time is that we all have enough. We really do. And when we use it properly, it seems as though we're gifted more. I once heard someone say that people are more effective throughout the day when they've started their day with a ritual that represents what's most-sacred, most fundamental in their life. For me, that would unequivocally be prayer. Starting the day with a prayer centers me and puts me in touch with what's needed. That's when I find the extra minutes.

The reality is, you don't have ten hours a day for your project. You may not even have 10 hours a week! But if you have the clarity and the inspiration, those hours will be enough to make it work. You'll be given the guidance you need to make it happen. Draw on inspiration. Stay in tuned. Start with the things that matter most, and you will get the guidance you need to make it all work in that time that you have.

Keep Family Time Uninterrupted

When Jennifer Sattley set out to create the stunning food blog Carlsbad Cravings, she implemented a practice that would prevent the new project from taking over her family time. Although she spent countless hours on the project, Jennifer explains that during family time, the computer and phone MUST be put away. Again, a simple habit with HUGE implications. During our interview, I asked her about whether her recipe posts on social media were a distraction, whether she felt compelled to check them multiple times throughout the day to see how they were doing. I know from personal experience that when a project is tied in with social media, time can quickly be consumed with update checks. I was curious as to how she handled this aspect of her business. She explained that early on in the project she made a decision to just *put them out there* and let them be. She realized that if she loved her posts, other people would probably love them too. She didn't need to follow up every hour of the day see how her Instagram, Pinterest, and Facebook posts were doing. Jennifer is a great example of an entrepreneur that knows how to keep her project work balanced!

Consider Your Time When Choosing a Project

Before you begin your project, consider how much of your time it will require. Even home-based businesses can leave you unavailable to your family if you're not careful. It's possible to create meaningful entrepreneurial projects that don't take up all of your time. Whether you've started a project that needs to be streamlined or simplified, or you're in the planning phase of a business startup, recognize the hours and minutes of your day as your most-valuable resource!

Rebecca Forbush is a fantastic example in this arena. The mother and canvas painter had become exhausted at a time-consuming business that had begun as something that she loved. While painting and selling canvas art is undoubtedly something that Rebecca was born to do, she could no longer justify the many hours it took to produce one painting. The time expenditure just wasn't worth the price tag of each piece. She wished she could continue making money somehow, doing something that she loved. By her third child, she knew that this venture had to close down.

Some time later, Rebecca was in need of a Christmas gift for a family member. She used her painting skills to whip out a family portrait in water color. It didn't take very long and the piece was a hit, so she did a few more. Before long, Rebecca realized that this was a way to produce a small income for her family while doing something that she loved. Unlike the canvas art, the watercolor family portraits could be produced in a shorter time period. She opened an Etsy shop and started selling the watercolor portraits.

Her shop became a huge hit when she entered the Instagram arena. She realized that this was a definite answer to prayer in many ways. With the Instagram networking platform, she was able to develop a large audience, product sales took off, and she was left with enough time to fulfill the other important roles in her life.

This is a great example in so many ways. It proves that we can find the best-possible solutions when we have an earnest desire and a willingness to prioritize. We must never forget how valuable our time is, particularly during this important phase in life.

Wrapping Up

We all have the same hours of the day. The way we choose to spend our time will ultimately determine the outcome of our lives. Our relationships, our beliefs, and our accomplishments are all developed as a result of the way we spend our time. The things that contribute to wise time expenditure:

- Give up a habit
- Add a habit
- Know how to multitask
- Realize the value of a purpose-centered day
- Institute a POWER HOUR
- Start your day with the things that matter
- Keep family time uninterrupted
- Consider your time when choosing a project

STEP 8

Declutter. Make Room for the Good Stuff

"We are infinitely more than our limitations or our afflictions!"
-Jeffrey R. Holland

So often, as we set out for change, we experience roadblocks. While project challenges are to be expected, it's important to recognize when we've placed unnecessary limitations on ourselves through various habits and mindsets. Emotional and spiritual clutter such as jealousy, pride, self-doubt, and criticism will swallow up this creative process. Habits of this nature threaten our strength, our ambition, and our ability to stay inspired. And even more so, they threaten our influence. When we feel inadequate, unqualified, or even fearful, we stand in our own way. Depending on how "messy" things have gotten, it may be impossible to become inspired, activate intention, or get organized! In this step, we'll identify ways to eliminate this kind of clutter. This is an extension of our conversation on "cultivation."

Norman Vincent Peale made a profound assertion regarding the topic of "effectiveness" in his moving bestseller, The Power of Positive Thinking (Yes, this again. It's that good). Peale discovered an insight on Thomas Edison's work patterns and his ability to maintain incredible focus. Edison's wife explained that the man was effective because he worked in harmony with nature and with God in this way:

"In him there were no obsessions, no disorganizations, no conflicts, no mental quirks, no emotional instability... He drew his energy from emotional self-mastery, the ability to relax completely. His amazingly harmonious relationship with the universe caused nature to reveal to him its inscrutable secrets."

So here's a question worth consideration: Could an inventor such as Thomas Edison have received such prolific inspiration if he were preoccupied with inadequacies, jealousies, or a quarrel with the neighbors? I doubt it. Think of what it would take to receive THAT kind of clarity.

I think that we often lose sight of what we're also capable of accomplishing. I'm not Thomas Edison or Mother Teresa, but the reality is, the influence of a single woman is more expansive than we can imagine. A mother's influence alone will span generations. Don't ever underestimate what you were born to do. Mental and spiritual clarity is just as vital for you as it was for Thomas Edison. Make this realization and then identify the clutter that's standing in the way

Acknowledge the Clutter

Here's an exciting prospect: You are about to eliminate the habits that are holding you back. This process will make you more creative, more inspired, and more successful in every area of your life. But in order to get started, you'll need to first acknowledge the clutter. We all have it. Here are some of the habits that are easy to slip into:

Feeling sorry for ourselves
Complaining
Competing
Comparing
Indulging in regular self-criticism

These are just a few. There are also a gaggle of them in the PRIDE department - *when we're not willing to admit our shortcomings or ask for help.* We all have clutter. Most of the time it hibernates within us waiting for that perfect moment to go tromping all over our big plans. But I believe that when we're ready to confront it, we witness a potential within ourselves that we never before imagined. Clutter interrupts the creative process and makes us unavailable to the people and the inspiration that we need. You can feel it as it happens, whether it's in the form of comparisons, negative self-talk, or a sense of fear that leaves you feeling paralyzed. Ultimately, the clutter hijacks our position as the author. If left unchecked, it begins to override the story that we would have written for ourselves. While this may present as an exaggeration, just think about those moments that you're consumed in clutter. You suddenly feel unqualified, apathetic, or even unworthy. So just recognize it – because you are worthy.

Habit Replacement Plan

If you've ever started a diet at the turn of the new year, you probably know how difficult it can be to change old habits. But take heart in knowing that it is possible. Behavioral psychologists agree that the BEST way to get rid of an unwanted habit is to replace it. In other words, find another thought, word, or action to replace the one that's holding you back. Set it up ahead of time so you know exactly what to do when you're faced with the negative habit. As you work through this process deliberately, you can actually choose actions that make you more inspired, more compassionate, and overall, a better person. In terms of your project, this process will give you the clarity that you need to become the vehicle to whatever endeavors you are inspired to pursue.

To illustrate how this can be done, I'll use the insidious habit of JEALOUSY as an example. I find this topic pertinent for the subject of entrepreneurship. Though common, feelings of jealousy are destructive. It stirs up feelings of self-doubt, defeat, and bitterness. We often feel it when we see others obtaining things that we wish we had. And jealousy is a tricky player. When we see things that should otherwise inspire us, a sense of jealousy often beats it to the punch. Instead of feeling inspired we feel down, hopeless, even angry. Jealousy is often the resistance we feel when we're faced with "what could be."

If there's any clutter worth going after, it's jealousy. Here's how the Habit Replacement Plan can work. The first step is to acknowledge jealousy (or another bad habit) whenever it comes up. Next, assign a deliberate replacement. In this case, we'll replace JEALOUSY with ENTHUSIASM. When feelings of jealousy arise, realize that you're only experiencing this feeling because you're facing something that inspires you! That's reason to get excited! Enthusiastic! Close your eyes and imagine how you would feel if that were your own achievement. Then, project those feelings to the person. At first, this may feel disingenuous, but who cares! This is going to make you better. You might also consider going a step further, following up with a physical gesture: a word of congratulation, a phone call, or email. The more tied up you've become in this emotion, the more you'll need to pour into the "replacement" process. Express your happiness for what that person has achieved! Get into the habit of producing immediate feelings of enthusiasm for other people's successes and you'll begin carving out your own success! Over time, these thoughts and gestures will become habits and your ability to feel joy for people will come naturally. Instead of feeling jealous, you will sense the abundance within your own life.

Jealousy is just one example of clutter. When we learn to change these kinds of habits, we are able to best-cultivate our intentions.

In the following portion of The Success Project you'll work to identify your commonly-used habits (your thoughts, words, and actions) and then decide whether they're pointing you in the right direction. Consider whether your thoughts, words, and actions represent the trajectory that you really want for your life.

If this experience is something that you're comfortable sharing with a friend, spouse, or family member, moral support may help you successfully implement these new changes. I've asked my daughter to help me get rid of my habit of complaining. We've first agreed on what it means to complain. Now, whenever my daughter senses a pointless rumination of some negative experience, she'll point it out. But at this point, I can generally sense a complaint before it comes out. When I'm on the ball, I'll modify my statement into a productive observation, OR just keep my mouth shut. Those are the two best replacement habits that I've come up with for that particular habit. You can implement this approach for anything. Again, it's easier to replace a habit with something else rather than just getting rid of it.

Before you begin, here are a few things to consider:

- How do you respond when faced with negative circumstances?
- Do your habits represent the intentions that you've set for your life?
- Do your habits properly cultivate the experiences that you desire for your life and the person you hope to become?

This is an incredibly personal experience – one for which you are also entitled direct inspiration. Pray for what you can change and seek inspired solutions.

You might consider working on just ONE habit at a time. And here's a concept, start with something simple. Like a debt elimination plan, when we begin by eliminating the smallest debt, there's more to contribute to the larger deficiencies.

Here's a list of habits to get you thinking:

Thoughts

Clutter	Replacement Habit
Doubting your abilities	Visualizing yours goals daily
Wishing for a better life	Strategically forming measurable goals and utilizing affirmations
Feeling stress, defeat, and resentment at others' successes	Project enthusiasm for others' successes
Criticizing the actions of others	Frequently giving people the benefit of the doubt
Feeling frustrated when your expectations are not met	Projecting love for the people in your life and recognizing the humanness in others
Feeling pride in what you've accomplished and taking ownership for what you've done without recognizing God as the source to every good thing	Exercising Humility – the act of recognizing that you are the not the source of your success. Recognizing God in all of your accomplishments
Feeling shame over lost opportunity	Feeling grateful for learning through challenges

Words

Clutter	Replacement Habit
Complaining	Expressing gratitude
Staying in your comfort zone	Showing interest in others, Starting conversation
Projecting blame	Speaking positively even in painful situations
Gossiping	Spreading good news
Expressing doubt	Finding something you're grateful about and vocalizing it to someone

Actions

Clutter	Replacement Habit
Watching television	Daily Meditation and Prayer
Social Media Habits	Journaling
Preparing to interject your ideas as others speak	Being an active listener, engaged in what other people have to say
Starting the day with lengthy media pass-times such as television or computer	Organizing responsibilities for the day and creating daily measurable goals
Staying in your comfort zone	Introducing yourself to strangers
Waiting to see what happens	Taking action
Maintaining a stance of being "too busy" for service to others.	Maximizing service opportunities when they arise
Time-consuming participation in unproductive activities such as TV and Internet	Daily learning and entertainment through positive sources

Wrapping Up

I believe that each of us has the potential to do amazing things, more than most of us can imagine. But we must be willing to look inward and ask ourselves... *am I prepared for what I set out for?* As we declutter and cleanse the inner vessel, we can become the vehicle something truly amazing.

Phase 4– Pressing Forward

STEP 9

Confront Project Challenges

"Our ultimate freedom is the right and power to decide how anybody or anything outside ourselves will affect us."
-Stephen Covey

I'm going to be really straight forward here as we delve into the topic of project challenges. First off, they'll be there. You can count on it. For one woman, it may be internal challenge, a sense of inadequacy or other areas of "clutter." For another, it may be physical obstacles related to the project itself. Whatever those challenges are, you can be assured that they will surface in one way or another as you pursue your project. It's just the nature of this thing. Whenever you set out to do something big, there will be resistance. But this is not necessarily a bad thing. As you experiences challenges, you're essentially forced to deal with whatever issues come up. Thanks to your project, you may now come face-to-face with these things that have probably been holding you back in other areas of your life. Regardless of the challenge, we must never forget that this is a story worth writing - or in the following analogy, a race worth running.

During a podcast interview hosted by Sheri Dew, Elaine Dalton described an experience that she had as she and her husband were running together. During a long and exhausting training session, Elaine was falling behind. As they came upon a difficult hill, she decided to quit. She called to her husband that she was going to head back to the car. She was exhausted and didn't think she could do any more. Her husband quickly turned back to her said something that she would never forget, *never stop when you're in the middle of a hill.* Elaine has since remembered that analogy as it applies in so many areas of "life."

We are all faced with hills of every kind. Those times of resistance are often the times that we want to throw in the towel! But the reality is, if we can traverse the hills, we can become something greater than we were before we began.

Based on my own experience and my research, these are some of the most common challenges for new entrepreneurs. These are some of the hills that you'll likely face. While this section of the book may seem a bit directive, I'll be honest in admitting that I'm here with you. Challenges are very much a part of my life. Much of the advice issued here is advice that I've been given and I continue to give myself. Please take heart in knowing that, for the most part, we're all in the same boat.

Self-Doubt

We tend to assume that everyone in life is just where they should be. Perhaps we believe that certain people are just somehow more innately worthy of their position in life. Whether they're professional, smart, decisive, empathetic, athletic, good with money... that's just how they are. We make assumptions about what "box" we fit into as well and then we maintain a trajectory of what we assume we're capable of. You might be a procrastinator because up until now, you've always procrastinated. Or maybe you're messy, hot-tempered, indecisive... Of course, because you've proven to yourself that it's who you are by living that way day after day. You are who you are and that's just the way it is. And that, my friend, is the lie. In the words of Ralph Waldo Emerson, *the only person you're destined to become is the person you decide to be.* Believe me, this can be tough. I think it's a work in progress for most of us, myself included - myself, especially. I think the trick to overcoming self-doubt is first realizing that we can decide to go in another direction – any direction. Here's something that I wish I could say to you face to face, eye to eye: You are capable of being whoever you want to be. Regardless of where you're from, what you've done, or what other people think of you, this is your story. Don't ever doubt your ability to write your own story.

Now, this is something that I really believe in. If you want to become something, you have to act like it. If you want to be an athlete, act like an athlete. If you want to be organized, act like someone who's organized. In other words, do the things that those people do. It may not feel natural at first, you may have no idea what you're doing, but eventually, those behaviors will become part of who you are.

At one point during my late-twenties when I was asked to manage a large event that involved a lot of work and a fair deal of conflict, I had to continually remind myself of this concept. So often, I'd find myself looking around thinking *what we need here is an adult in charge – someone to make adult decisions.* I kid you not, there were so many points during that experience that I had to say to myself *Ok, Elisha, just do whatever a mature adult in this situation would do.* To this day, I find myself doing the same thing. *How would a really good parent handle this conflict with their teenager? How would a decisive person handle this situation?*

My husband was in *his* twenties when he first stepped into a project management position at a large utility company. I would definitely describe him as a confident person, but there were also definite moments of hesitation as he moved into that leadership role. There were several directors in the company that he really looked up to. I watched as he often asked for advice and then modeled their professionalism. At times he would even save another employee's well-written email to refer back to – again, something to model. At first, he didn't see himself as a corporate manager, but over time and with practice, it became part of him.

It's normal to doubt ourselves. But sitting and stewing over what is possible (or not seemingly possible) will only aggravate the situation. We must be willing to jump in to that new role and start playing the part! To do this, you'll first need to meet people who are already doing it. What are their features? What are they doing that inspires you?

When I interviewed Jill Thomas she mentioned that "getting outside of yourself" is often the key to getting inspired. We learn so much from watching others. She explained that she'd often talked with artists who were struggling with inspiration and feeling stuck. This is always her recommendation – *get outside of yourself*. This is the very reason that I interviewed two-dozen women for this project! I wanted to showcase the features of these amazing women, their characteristics, the way that they interact with others, the way they "do business." These women are truly inspiring! If we can make observations about how it's done, we can glean these qualities. We can learn how to reach beyond ourselves and become more than we are today. Through this process, we begin to believe in the story that we're creating.

Competition

This is such a common challenge. And we're conditioned to believe that it's okay to go with it! Expressions such as "healthy competition" or "squash the competition" have been assimilated into this world of entrepreneurship. It seems harmless, until you break it down to what it really means. To compete with another means to try to *get ahead.* Meaning, someone is left behind. So the goal in a competition is to GET AHEAD and leave others behind. How, in any way possible, could this be a positive mindset for anyone? From my perspective, we cultivate GREATNESS in ourselves when we cultivate greatness in others. Starting a business not only takes drive, it takes incredible vulnerability. We all start from the same starting line. If we view others as our "competition," we're missing the biggest point. Those *others* are the strength. If they're more experienced, we can gain wisdom from them. We become the best of ourselves when we reach to others for inspiration. Here's a lesson that my mom taught me when I was a young dancer... *"There will always be someone ahead of you and always someone behind."* We're all growing at our own pace. If we can learn to emulate others' strengths, and strengthen those who need us, we'll all get there.

Now, in terms of your project, there are some practical reasons to erase the concept of competition from your mind. First and foremost, networking. If you're considering a market that requires a social media presence, a competitive vibe is not a good approach. In order to build your social media presence, you must have support from others. When you have a competitive mindset, you're less likely to promote others, less likely to emulate great ideas, and frankly, you're less likeable too.

When I hung up the phone after speaking Jennifer Sattley, I thought to myself... She has ZERO EGO, really. She seems to have no sense of competition, whatsoever. When she sees other successful business concepts like hers, she feels an immediate sense of happiness and enthusiasm, never feeling threatened or inadequate. That state of humility has, no doubt, prepared her to receive inspiration for her project. She is like an open vessel, ready and waiting for inspiration to pour over her. Her blog, Carlsbad Cravings is evidence of that.

When we feel threatened by someone else's success, we cheat ourselves of an opportunity for growth. When you feel a sense of competition, identify what threatens you and recognize it as something that you can also achieve! Add it to your intention list. Little by little, that's how you'll get to where you're inevitably headed!

Fear

Fear is a very typical challenge, one that we can all expect to experience at one time or another. But the goal should not be to remove fear from the equation rather, to move forward in spite of fear. Let your faith be BIGGER than your fear! That is called courage. When you move courageously through the uncomfortable portions of your project, you become stronger. Here are some perspectives that have helped me deal with my own fears:

Know that it's Natural

Fear is just one of the amazing human experiences. The adrenaline produced from fear can actually be the perfect ingredient for a public speech, stage performance, or even a negotiation. When you experience fear, it's because you are human, NOT because you are weak. When we venture into uncharted territories, we can expect to feel some discomfort. I've heard, so often, that when you're headed in the right direction, things will feel good! And that is absolutely true in most cases. However, I can honestly say that many of my best decisions have scared me. When I make the decision to confront it, whatever it is, I can almost feel myself growing into my true potential. Whatever it is that you're afraid of now - writing the email, making the phone call, asking for help – keep in mind that there may be something really awesome on the other side of that fear. Sometimes, the greatest things in life come with greatest resistance. Just imagine what you could accomplish if fear didn't stand in your way.

Embrace It

While it may seem crazy, resisting fear is the worst thing you can do. Have you ever been terrified on a roller coaster? The best thing you can do to alleviate your panic is to scream! That will likely not work so well in a board room, but when you're scared, don't be afraid to address it. Share your concerns with a confidant so you can air it out! During one particular project of mine, I was secretly dreading the moment that my project would come to fruition. I felt incredibly vulnerable. During a phone conversation with a relative I expressed that I was terrified of my project unveiling. That conversation was an immediate antidote to my fears. Simply saying, "I'm terrified" lightened my burden.

Choose Courage

Use the habit replacement plan to change that fear to courage! As you consider the project at hand, dwell on your enthusiasm for the end result to push through those scary or intimidating times. When I interviewed artist, Rebecca Forbush, she was open about the fear factor that existed for her during the beginning phases of her project. She described that sense of inferiority that came up as she considered who to contact to during the initial phases of social media networking. She knew that her Instagram account would be a great way to build her business, but felt a little scared about putting herself out there. But after reaching out to several people and making some great milestones on Instagram, she realized that it was worth it to push through the fear! She explained, "The worst thing someone can do is say 'no', or ignore you." This "worst case scenario" approach is a really a great way to analyze your risks. Are you afraid because you stand to lose something? Or are you just afraid of what someone will think of you? Decide what you're really afraid of and make an inspired decision to more forward. Don't allow your fears to stop you in your tracks!

Break Fears with Experience

We can overcome almost any fear with practice. The more we do something, the easier it becomes. So when something is difficult to confront, CONFRONT IT! Very few people could stand in front of a large group and speak without fear. But for a seasoned speaker, there's nothing to it! That's because they've done it countless times and they've become confident. The same goes for job interviews, auditions, or marketing phone calls! The more you do it, the better you'll become, and the less fearful you'll be. Whatever it is that's scaring you, consider confronting it now.

Procrastination

As the mother of 3 kids, this topic is the enduring source of many lectures in my house! Although it's also really common, it can be a deal-breaker for your project if you're not careful. When we put things off over and over again, we find ourselves buried in obligation and overwhelm.

Here are some tried and true ways to address and conquer the challenge of procrastination:

Make a MASTER LIST

I heard an organization expert refer to this practice and I just love it. Choose a wall space that you pass frequently throughout the day and hang a white board, a chalk board, or poster with the following three column titles:

<u>Today</u>   <u>This Week</u>   <u>This Month</u>

In each column, pinpoint your action items that should be completed within that respective time frame. This list should include those things that you might otherwise procrastinate. Perhaps it's laundry, a phone call, a thank you card, or reviewing with a child for a spelling test. Those longer-term items tend to be the most easily procrastinated. But if they're on your MASTER LIST, you'll see them each day and be more likely to get them done!

Delegate

This concept is extremely helpful in running a household. If household responsibilities are getting ahead of you, itemize tasks and assign action items to the members of your household rather than putting them off. In terms of your project, consider your resources and outsource when possible.

Disorganization

Disorganization is a challenge that most of us have to face. If I had a dollar for every mom who's said to me, "I have Adult A.D.D." I BELIEVE YOU! I'm pretty sure that I have it too! That's not the end of the road. It doesn't have to be a deal breaker for your project, as long as you create habits to overcome it. The reality is, many successful people are not naturally organized. I believe that disorganization is a typical trait for creative minds. So, if you're not naturally organized, know that you're normal and get organized anyway.

My first suggestion (speaking from experience) is to take account of your time on your phone or computer. It's hard to organize your life when your brain is working on overdrive and that's exactly what I experience when I've had too much screen time. Think about it - the way that our brain conducts itself in front of a digital interface is unlike any other experience humans have had in history. We experience immediate response with the click of a finger and our brain has become accustomed to these speedy conditions. It makes the daily, mundane tasks seem stagnant and arduous. In these modern days, maintaining focus takes work. Before delving into other ways to become organized, first consider how much time you're inadvertently devoting to your phone or computer. Those are a death trap for the already-cluttered mind. Allow yourself certain periods of the day (maybe before bed or first thing in the morning) to check email, or update your status.

Here are some other tips for keeping things together:

Set Your Timer

If you tend to fall into tasks and forget about the world around you, USE YOUR TIMER. Every smart phone has one. A timer also comes in handy for chores that seem insurmountable. Assign yourself to 15 minutes of something. A timer can be a great resource for someone that's not naturally organized. You can remind yourself of when to start, when to stop, and when to run out the door to pick up the kids from school!

Create the Space

Designate a specific place for your thoughts and your action items. Organize your work space as well. Have a place for bills, keepsakes, items of importance, and your ideas. Creating a physically organized space can help you maintain metal focus.

Don't Skip Between Action Items

Have you ever known a really task-oriented person? They tend to get a lot done and I believe it's from a habit of moving down that task list, completing things one item at a time. They don't skip around from one item to another. This may sound like a no-brainer here, but it's important to remember. By way of example, when I'm toward the end of my content development phase for a new website, it's often a temptation to begin browsing for accompanying photo stock, social media venues, or link possibilities. But the reality is, this will greatly slow the writing portion of the project. When I jump between tasks, my focus is diluted and the initial action item takes longer and is often insufficient. Instead, it's best to zero in on the task at hand until it is scraped dry BEFORE moving down the list.

Chronic Discouragement

Chronic discouragement is a challenge that can be devastating in more ways than one. I'm not talking about a discouraging day, we all have those. I'm talking about real, true, CHRONIC discouragement – when we can't get past that hopeless mindset: *Why aren't things panning out? Why do things always go wrong? Nothing I do is good enough.* I'll be honest in admitting that I personally struggle with this one from time to time. One day (during a particularly gloomy season) when I was reading my scriptures, I came across a few verses in the book Matthew that awakened my mind to a new perspective. This section of scripture references the "salt of the Earth." I realized in that moment that the "salt of the Earth" is a wonderful role to play. SALT flavors everything it touches. It makes bland things taste better. It helps us *eat* those life-sustaining vegetables that would otherwise taste awful. Salt is wonderful. It's a blessing. When I read these words, I realized two things. First, I want to be the salt of the Earth. That's a role that I desire and I believe it is the role that God has for me, just as He has for you. Secondly, when I am in a state of chronic discouragement, I lose my savor. I'm no longer available as a listener, a counselor, a cheerleader, or in the other ways that I bless others. I am all-encompassed by the discouragement that is stealing away my opportunity to write my story. Take note the next time you're feeling down and make every effort to move past it! Be faithful in the face of discouragement and realize that your life is a great influence to others. Don't allow a little doubt or a little failure to steal away your savor.

Mistakes

There may be no greater teaching experience in the world than our own mistakes. At times, project-building can feel like a never-ending series of them. When we decide to make those "big moves," mistakes are almost inevitable. When entrepreneur, Dianna Barton started basket company, Plum & Sparrow, she drew on her past business ventures as a resource for her future success. As she considered her previous business experiences, she recognized the mistakes she'd made, which avenues she missed, and ultimately, what she needed to do to make the new venture fly. To this day, she doesn't look at those past ventures as "failures" but rather, the resources that have brought her to where she is today.

Negative Opinions

"Their opinion of you is none of your business." This is life advice from my dad. And it's good, oh so good. The reality is, everyone has an opinion and not everyone will agree with yours. In fact, IF everyone agrees with you, you might be doing something wrong. When you are brave enough to join the race, you can be assured that opinions will arise and they won't all be nice. It happens to ALL OF US! Negativity doesn't need to define us! If you have platform, know that some will love you and others will not. I learned this concept first hand when I decided to open a YouTube channel for my nutrition blog, Motivated Mamas. It was just a hobby for me after having my third child. I hosted a few weight loss challenges, and as a result of the experience, ended up doing a certification program in nutrition. I thought it would be fun to add a YouTube channel to my repertoire! I was thrilled when the videos started gaining traffic! One of them had over 32,000 views. I decided to look through the comments on those videos to see what my viewers thought of it! This may have been a mistake, but I was really serious about getting feedback. While some of the comments were encouraging – *You're darling. I love your apron. This video is super helpful.* – the first comment (very first) read: *Oh my gosh I can't handle her voice.* The second comment read: *No joke. Great info but her voice is like nails on a chalkboard.* When I shared this story with a trusted group of friends, one pointed out that I do have a distinct personality, one that some people will adore, and others might hate. (I'm not sure she really said HATE, but that was the gist of it). And you know what? She's right! The reality is, if you try to conform to make everyone happy, you'll lose yourself in the process. Be true to who you are and remember that this is your journey, your story! Stay true to who you are and what you stand for. Some will love it, some will hate it, and that's the way it always goes.

Game-Changers

While we're on the topic of "challenges," I'd be remised if I failed to mention the ultimate adversity – the thing we all hate to face: the game changer. Maybe you haven't heard this expression. I suppose it's a positive take on an otherwise frustrating, disappointing, or even devastating circumstance. While this may sound entirely too depressing for our topic of project building, I think it's imperative that we discuss it for a few reasons. First, we all face game changers and it's important to know that when you're experiencing one, you're not alone. Secondly, the way we react to a game-changer means more than I can say. Before we go any further, let me describe what a game-changer is in my book: When you dream big, plan your brains out, and make every possible effort to plan your life and... things don't go your way, that's a game changer. It means that there is something else in store for you. There are pieces to the puzzle that you don't see. The game isn't OVER, it's just changed. Sometimes this happens to protect us or to direct us to something better. But I suspect that in many cases, we don't actually know why.

A major game-changer happened in my life after I completed a build-out for a new performing arts studio. I had made the announcement to more than a hundred students, spent an entire summer in construction, and even discontinued my contract in my prior studio space. But soon after the build-out was complete, city zoning laws changed and I wasn't able to use the new space. Ultimately, the entire operation closed down. I had planned, worked tirelessly, and poured all of my financial resources into this project and it suddenly came crashing down. I was devastated. I felt like a complete failure. I begged the Lord to help me figure it out but I knew it was over. At that point, I prayed for peace. I eventually found a sweet and strange serenity through that experience. I didn't understand why it panned out that way, but like many of the other inspired ideas that have visited me through the years, this experience also left me with a calm and collected peace of mind.

Every once in a while we get to see the other side of a game-changer –*why* things changed the way they did. Not always, but when it happens, it's remarkable. When a brilliant friend of mine didn't get into nursing school, we were all surprised. It was a definite game changer that she couldn't understand. A few weeks later she found out that she was pregnant. Had she actually been accepted, it would have been nearly impossible to complete a P.A. nursing program with a new baby. She didn't get into the program because someone was watching out for her and she knew it. We've spoken about this topic at length, how often *life* happens in ways we don't expect. "Can you imagine doing all of this alone?" I remark. Her come-back was perfect, "My life would be in shambles." Yep, mine too. I guess it's a good thing that we're not making all of these decisions on our own.

Another friend of mine had always looked forward to the day that she would be a stay-at-home parent – once her husband was established in his career. But she couldn't get past an ongoing impression that she needed to go to graduate school. It wasn't part of her plan but she eventually made the decision to follow that inspiration and was accepted to the program of her choice. The following couple of years presented challenges that were often more than she'd bargained for. Her life consisted of 2-hour drives to her school campus, a heavy course load, and of course, a continuation of her duties at home, which included being a mother to two small kids. But through it all she continued to reflect on that clear direction she had received to go to graduate school, so she continued.

The reason for this inspired "game-changer" eventually became clear. During that time, her husband had a serious injury which over several years developed into a debilitating brain and neurological disorder. The physically disabling progression was such that he had to eventually discontinue full-time work, then discontinue part-time work, until finally, he was no longer able to work, drive a car, or walk without assistance. This faithful family suddenly knew the purpose of that inspired direction over the previous few years. For many years to come, my friend was able to support her family financially, thanks to that graduate degree. When we're prepared to listen and respond to inspired direction, we can face the "game-changers" of life with conviction, courage, and faith.

The important thing to remember is this: game-changers are not a reason to stop writing. I believe that in every case, these unexpected plot twists will lead to a fantastic story development if we will continue writing. In those tough situations, I think most of us would rather throw down the pen and scratch the whole thing. But that's when we must recognize that a reckoning is in order. There are big questions that we must be willing to ask: What will come of it? Will it shape me? Will it change me? Where will I go from here? In some cases, the formidable game-changer proves to be the catalyst to a brave new chapter.

In a web video series called "How I Share It," blogger and Instagram personality, Alison Faulkner of *The Alison Show* describes the impact of a life-changing event that ultimately led to a pretty amazing career. That "life-changing event" was the day that her husband lost his job. In the interview, Alison describes that day. The couple shared a long embrace, followed by a mutual resolve that they'd both delve into their *gifts* as a new source of income for their family. They were devastated, no doubt. But that day was a turning point. They made a decision to move forward. The couple soon began building their own businesses: The Alison Show and Pleasant Pictures Music; both have flourishes. Alison has been featured by Martha Stewart, she has TENS of thousands of followers on Instagram, and she spreads the message of self-acceptance, passion, and creativity through her spunky and inspiring video blog, The Alison Show. This couple's game-changer led to bright new opportunity – something that perhaps they never saw coming. Just imagine how easy it would have been to allow the job-loss to derail them. It was, in fact, the catalyst to a beautiful new storyline.

When singer and songwriter Calee Reed experienced the most painful moment of her life, the death of her mother, her life also took a new course. Up until that point, she loved music, wrote music, and performed often. But during her mother's illness, Calee discovered her passion for the Christian music genre. She relied on it to get through that most-challenging time in her life. After her mother passed away, Calee made a decision to pursue Christian music as a career. She obtained a recording contract and released her first album which beautifully depicted her mother's life and her influence. Calee continues to work as a recording artist and travels as an inspirational speaker. Calee has used the most difficult experience in her life to fuel her passion for music and to bless the lives of others through her remarkable gift.

In the words of C.S. Lewis, "Hardships often prepare ordinary people for an extraordinary destiny" I suppose it's all in the way we allow those hardships (those game-changers) to influence us.

Wrapping Up

There are many possible challenges that you'll face as you pursue your project. Here are some of the common challenges that every mompreneur should be aware of:

- ## Competition
   Erase it
    It doesn't need to exist
   We're all in it together
   Network
   Love others

- ## Fear
   It's normal
   Embrace it
   Transform it
   Choose Courage
   Break it with experience

- ## Procrastination
   Make list
   First things first
   Delegate

- ## Disorganization
   Make lists visible
   Set a timer

Create the space

Don't skip between action items

- Self-Doubt

Be faithful

Strength comes from God, not you

Never quit when you are in the middle of a hill

- Mistakes

Learn from them

Continue moving forward

- Negative Opinions

We don't have to be influenced by them. They don't change who we are or what we're doing in life. If you're brave enough to get inside the ring, you can expect people to say something about it.

- Game Changers

When things don't go the way you plan, there's another plan.

STEP 10

Cross the Finish Line

This last and final step presented here was initially entitled to represent the finish line of your project venture. Before I began writing, I brainstormed the steps involved in starting a home-based business and I wanted the final step to tie up the pieces of your project journey. But after a little consideration, I recognized that in most cases, our projects don't necessarily meet a finish line. I vacillated on whether to even include this last step. But the more that I thought about it, the more I recognized that our lives are a culmination of projects of every kind. Every role that we hold in life contributes itself to a colorful collaboration. The project of motherhood, the project of entrepreneurship, friendship, stewardship... the list goes on. After writing the details of this mompreneur manual, I realize that the finish line represents more than the end of your "project." It is something much more sacred. It signifies the final product – YOU. You are the subject of this great race. The finish line is where you're headed.

Some time ago my friend, Jamie Pyatt, entered an Ironman triathlon. Even for a seasoned triathlete, the Ironman is an extreme physical challenge most of us would consider too difficult to attempt. In my friend's case, she was already a runner, a swimmer, and she was pretty comfortable on a bike, but when her brother challenged her to this colossal goal, she knew that she'd need an advanced training schedule. Her preparation began with relatively small steps. Day one included something like 20 minutes of running and biking. Each consecutive day it became a little more rigorous. Every training day leading up to that race she made a concerted effort to prepare. She put one foot in front of the other. She bicycled the biggest hills in her town, swam, and ran regularly – everything that she needed to do to prepare for the big day. When she tells this story, she is clear about this point: the training didn't happen all at once. It was a steady slope of daily choices that amounted to her final preparation.

When the day of the big race finally arrived, Jamie was distraught to find that her brother, who was also her race partner, would be unable to compete with her. He was sick and there was nothing anyone could do. She would have to race alone.   Amidst her disappointment and a little fear, she gathered her composure and made her way to the starting line.

During that race, there were blisters, cramps, tears, and moments of desperate discouragement. But just as she did during her training, she chose to put one foot in front of the other. By the last 5-mile stretch of the run, Jamie could hear the names of the finishing contestants being announced over the loud speaker as they crossed the finish line. She continued to run as each name was called. During the last few painful miles she found herself running alongside a group of fire-fighters, racing in full, heavy uniform to raise money for charity.   They encouraged each other to keep moving. Finally, worn and wearied, Jamie made it to the finish line. She received her medal – she was a finisher.

At the same time that she was finishing the race, another woman was there receiving her 1st-place trophy. It had been hours since she'd crossed the finish line. During that time, the woman had actually gone home, taken a shower, gotten dressed, gone out to dinner and was finally back for the big announcement. And while she received her 1st place trophy, there was Jamie, *a finisher* - a sweaty, exhausted, and accomplished finisher. She was not there to be first or second; she was there for the race. She was there to finish.

When Jamie shared this story with a group of young women, she referenced a phrase of scripture that parallels the journey that led to her big finish. The beginning of this verse says "choose ye this day..." Jamie explains that regardless of the day, the verse always says the same thing. If you read it today it says "choose ye this day..." If you read it tomorrow it says "choose ye *this day*..." Every single day... we must choose.

As we embark on this chosen journey, we must each choose what we'll make of it. Every day is a new opportunity to make a new start. Regardless of whether you are running next to a first-place runner, a size-2 runner, or the "perfect mom" runner, this is your journey and yours alone. Today you may choose to walk. Tomorrow you may sprint. Some days, you may crawl. Each day is yours to choose. This is your race, your one and only race. Keep going until you cross the finish line.

The Final Wrap-up

With the tools and resources that are available in this modern digital age, it really seems possible to "have it all." Anyone with the right game-plan and a smartphone can make their business dream a reality. But let's not get swept away. Before setting out to make your project a *success*, consider what that word really means to you. As you map out the features of your plan, be assured that your picture of *success* is reflected in your formula. Be careful not to push ferociously ahead with your project venture thinking that "one day" it will all be worth it. "One day" those little people will be gone with lives of their own. They'll be busy. And what you'll have left is the legacy that you've created. Will it be a legacy of busyness? A legacy of appointments? Or will it be the legacy that God has laid out for you?

As my mom once expressed, the heroes of life are not necessarily the heroes of Heaven. That insight has spoken volumes to me through the years as I've pursued my projects. I'm reminded that in spite of grandiose ideas for new businesses, our biggest successes will not be in the form of website visitors, fan mail, Instgram followers, product sales, or interviews. Our greatest successes will likely take place on a small scale and probably within the walls of our own homes. If we can do one thing correctly, we'll remain in-tuned to that divine, loving guidance from our Father in Heaven so that we can pursue projects that really matter and never forget what's important.

In 2012, my friend, Jill Thomas, lost her sweet young daughter, Penny. For a person who's lived to see a child go before them, there's often a discernable awareness of what's most important in life. That is the case for Jill. After Penny's passing Jill had to redefine her role as a business owner. At first, she lost every ambition to continue as a photographer; it just seemed trivial in comparison to the more sacred fibers of her life that she was now so intimately in tuned to. But as months and years of grief and healing ensued, she recognized that Penny's entire life was recorded in photographs, even more than the rest of their children. Those images represent the precious moments of her family's life, their history, their memories, and the emotions that they've experienced together. As Jill studied those images of sweet Penny, she identified a new, transcendent purpose for her photography business. She realized that her work was a means to preserve those moments in life – for her family, and for others. Suddenly, her photography business stood for something much bigger.

Jill eventually made the decision to continue as photographer, this time, formulating a new project: a photography workshop series that would teach others how to beautifully document the moments of their own family lives. Jill's *Photos for Life Workshop* represents a convergence of her own purpose, passion, priority, and above all, inspiration. And that, my friend, is what this book is about.

The Success Project: 10 Steps for the Mompreneur was written for the purpose of helping mothers achieve the project dream, and every other earthly endeavor, through the process of divine inspiration. It is absolutely the main ingredient. By allowing Him to work through us, we can discover our own special purpose, fortify those around us, and achieve all of the most important *successes* of our lives.

THE SUCCESS STARTPACK

The Success Project is a title that is indicative of something much more than worldly "success." It is about cultivating the most important dimensions of our lives through worthy endeavors. Through our "projects" we can fortify those around us and develop a greater purpose for our own lives.

-The Success Project, 10 Steps for the Mompreneur

Dear Friend,

You are about to begin your own success project and I couldn't be more excited for you! I've designed The Success Startpack as an aid to help you get your project off the ground! I've included space for the personal evaluation and brainstorming exercises mentioned in The Success Project. Get your pen ready, you are about to make your project dream a real-life success.

If you prefer to use a printable version of The Success Startpack, you can find it at TheSuccessProject.com.
Best of Luck!!

Positively,

Elisha

Come find me on Instagram @ElishaExon and use the hashtag #SPCOLLAB to show off your progress! Can't wait to see you!

Introduction

The content included here in the Success Startpack is taken directly from The Success Project: 10 Steps for the Mompreneur and is intended for those who have already read the book. If you prefer to download a PDF version of the Success Startpack, visit TheSuccessProject.com for a free copy.

Set Your Intention

Your intention is your LANDING PLACE for this thing! In the words of Stephen Covey, "BEGIN WITH THE END IN MIND." This is important!! You will discover the necessary parts when you FIRST identify what you want. Think about where you want to be in 5, 10, or 20 years and jot down your thoughts here:

_____

_____

_____

_____

_____

_____

Identify Your Vision

Start here with your vision statement for your project. What is your goal? Be prayerful during this process and don't be afraid to be specific.

What I want:

_____

_____

_____

_____

_____

_____

_____

_____

_____

_____

_____

_____

_____

_____

Motivation

Describe why you want to achieve this goal. There may be more than one reason. It may be for money, prestige, honor, respect, stability... Whatever the reason is, be honest, identify it.

Why I want it:

———————————————————————

———————————————————————

———————————————————————

———————————————————————

———————————————————————

———————————————————————

———————————————————————

———————————————————————

———————————————————————

———————————————————————

———————————————————————

———————————————————————

———————————————————————

Purify Your Motive

It's essential that you identify a pure, solid motive for achieving your goal, something that you can feel proud of. Remember the example of the person trying to lose weight. When "looking hot" is the motive, the person may be conflicted with fears regarding pride, unwanted attention, and attracting the wrong things. When the motive becomes pure, then the goal is more worthy of fighting for. It starts when the motive is transferred to a purer place: health, energy, family time. Purify your motive by identifying the best reasons to achieve it. Think about how this goal will improve your life and improve the lives of others.

My purified motive for the project:

_____

_____

_____

_____

_____

_____

Amplify Your Intention

→ *The Bucket List*

Form a list of everything you want to accomplish in your life. Items on this list can be as practical or extravagant as you can imagine. Your list should include experiences or things that appeal to you, your desires. That may include vacations, humanitarian activities, creative projects, family experiences, career goals... anything that you want before you die, LIST IT. Let the world around you be your guide. Nothing is off limits.

Start your bucket list now! Write down the experiences that you want for your life

_____

_____

_____

_____

_____

_____

_____

_____

→Verbal Affirmations

Another approach to amplifying your intention is to declare your vision out loud, as if you've already achieved it. This is called a verbal affirmation. This technique is prescribed by countless success enthusiasts and teachers because it really works. The idea is to program the mind, convincing oneself of what is possible. In an article entitled, The Wise Open Mind Psychologist, Ronald Alexander Ph.D., states:

The mind doesn't know the difference between what is real or fantasy. When you watch a movie and your start to laugh or cry your mind is empathizing with the characters on the screen even though it is only Hollywood magic.

In the same way that our minds can be tricked into feeling grief, excitement, fear, or happiness for a character in a movie, we can likewise trick the mind into believing that something is achievable. The human brain has a miraculous way of solving problems. The reticular activating system decides which information is pertinent and necessary to any given situation. When you're driving a car, this part of your brain allows you to tune certain things out, while paying attention to things that are pertinent to your experience as a driver - sirens, stops lights, horns, turning signals. The reticular activating system provides a way to filter out all of the unnecessary information so that you can perform well in whatever you're doing. If you create a scenario and verbalize it as if it's true, that scenario becomes believable to the mind. Then, the reticular activating system will provide the information necessary to make that scenario true. So, whether you say I CAN or I CAN'T, you are right. Your mind will provide whatever information is necessary to create that reality. Never say anything about yourself that you wouldn't want to be true!

This experience of reciting daily affirmations can be very powerful when coupled with the corresponding emotion of gratitude. When you declare a desired experience as something you're grateful for already achieving, you send a powerful message to your mind! That positive state of gratitude will accelerate your intention!

These affirmations should absolutely be paired with your written declarative statements. Look at them often. Say them often. Design specific affirmations that reflect your desires for the future and say them each day.

Write a few affirmations to recite each day:
I am grateful that I

_____

_____

_____

I am grateful that I

_____

_____

_____

I am grateful that I

_____

_____

_____

I am grateful that I

_____

_____

_____

I am grateful that I

_____

_____

_____

I am grateful that I

_____

_____

_____

I am grateful that I

_____

_____

_____

I am grateful that I

_____

_____

_____

Build a Priority-Based Work Schedule

Before building your schedule, identify the areas of your life that need attention. When you complete the most important responsibilities first, you will find that you're able to complete more everywhere, including your project. With this in mind, it's important to identify which areas of your life hold the highest value for you.

Start by just considering the core dimensions of your life: spiritual, familial, emotional, marital, social, physical, financial, and intellectual. Decide which areas are most important and jot them down in the diagram.

- Spiritual
- Familial
- Marital
- Social

- Emotional
- Physical
- Financial
- Intellectual

Then, next to each respective "dimension," write down the contributions that you make within each area. For "familial", this could include meal planning, carpools, family councils, prayer time, meal time... For spiritual, it might include personal meditation, prayer, church service... Think about those areas and jot down each one in the diagram provided.

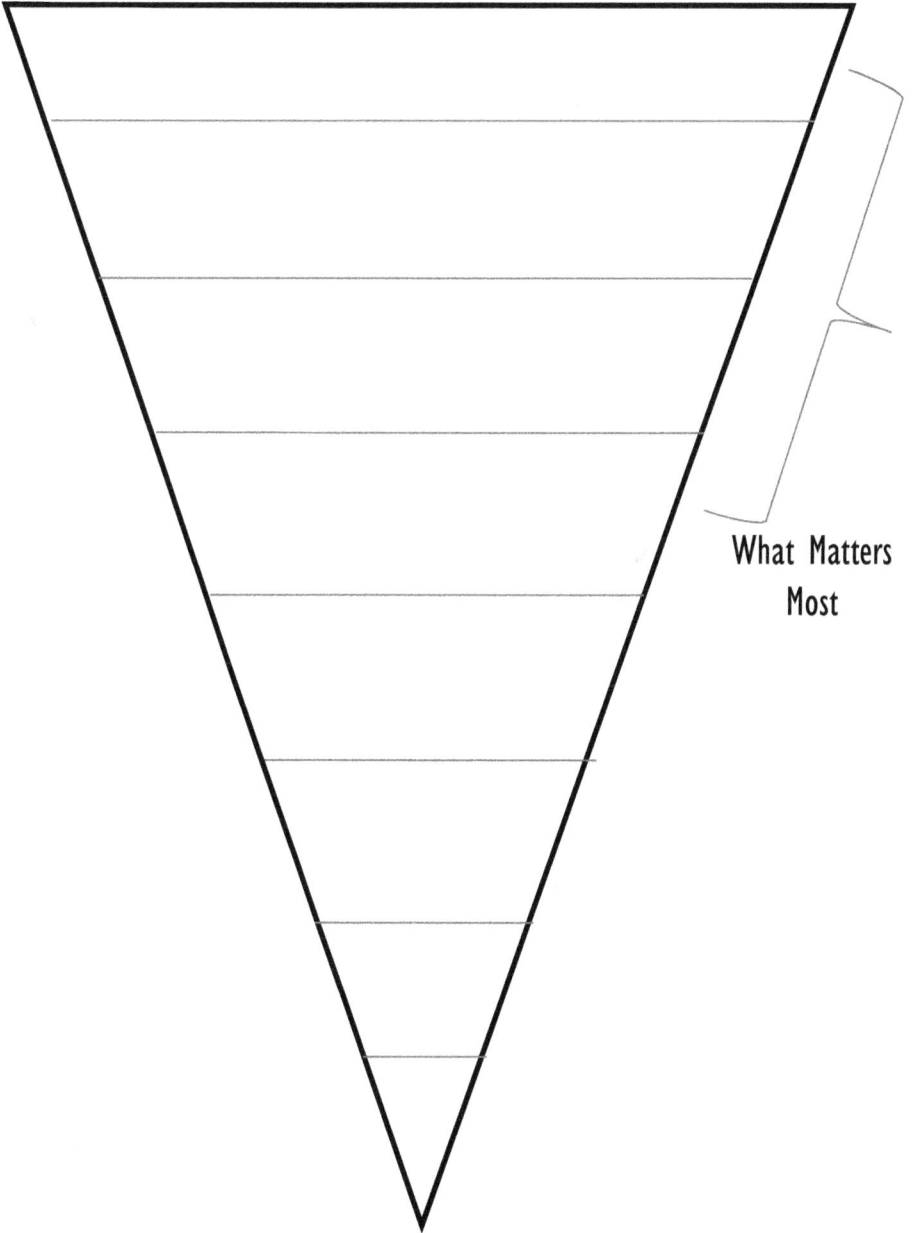

What Matters
Most

This step should bring these dimensions to life. It should help you see that even your seemingly mundane daily tasks are also an important part of the big picture. This will become relevant next, as you draw up your priority-based work schedule. Here's the basic idea: Each contribution to your life should be done deliberately, with that particular dimension in mind. When you're on a date night, recognize that as a contribution to the health of your marriage. When you're bathing the kids, recognize that as a contribution to your role as a mother. These are not meaningless experiences, they're an investment in something bigger! These experiences should never be diluted with project distractions: emails, Instagram posts, phone calls, or status updates. These are the areas that matter most! When you have those experiences, make the deliberate, let them mean something, and be present for them!

Delineate Your Responsibilities

Here's another space to jot down your responsibilities in each area of your life. Think about your roles: mom, wife, friend, tutor, teacher, room parent, school board member... write each one down and include the mandatory tasks associated with each one:

Role Title	Associated Obligations
Mother	*Caregiver, driver, cook, nurturer, counselor, friend*

Once those daily necessities are laid out, you're ready to carve out space for your project. This will likely require you to eliminate some of your current pastimes - television, social media, et cetera. You may also want to consider waking up earlier in the morning in order to work on your project. Consider school time, nap time, and any other spaces available during the day. This process will make you aware of what you have time for!

Accounting for each hour of your day is important for a few reasons. First off, you'll have a firm sense of accountability in terms of your time expenditure. You'll be less likely to waste time on senseless tasks: getting lost in the social media loop, checking your email, or surfing around on Pinterest. Instead, you'll use your designated "check social media" time that you've allocated for yourself. Other times during the day will be devoted to other important obligations. With this perspective, you'll be more inclined to use that time wisely!

Here's an example of a mom/boss schedule. You'll see that certain blocks of time have multiple obligations listed. I've found that I can get a lot done in a single hour. Take a look, then sketch out your own schedule on the following page.

	Mon	Tues	Wed	Thur	Fri
6am	Exercise Scripture Prayer	Exercise Scripture Prayer	Exercise Scripture Prayer	Exercise Scripture Prayer	Exercise Scripture Prayer
7am	Ready For School	Ready For School	Ready For School	Ready For School	Ready For School
8am	Carpool	Carpool	Carpool	Carpool	Carpool
9-12	Gavin & Mom	Gavin & Mom	Gavin & Mom	Gavin & Mom	Gavin & Mom
12-3	**WORK**	**WORK**	**WORK**	**WORK**	**WORK**
3pm	Carpool	Carpool	Carpool	Carpool	Carpool
4pm	Homework	Homework	Homework	Homework	Friends
5pm	Dinner Family Time	Dinner Family Time	Dinner Family Time	Dinner Family Time	Pizza & Date Night
6pm	Power Hour	Power Hour	Power Hour	Power Hour	Date Night
7pm	FAMILY NIGHT	Down Time	Down Time	Down Time	Date Night
8pm	Prayer Story Bedtime	Prayer Story Bedtime	Prayer Story Bedtime	Prayer Story Bedtime	Prayer Story Bedtime
9pm	Elective	Elective	Elective	Elective	Elective
10pm	Elective	Elective	Elective	Elective	Elective
10:30	Sleep	Sleep	Sleep	Sleep	Sleep

								Mon
								Tues
								Wed
								Thu
								Fri
								Sat
								Sun

Idea Throw-down

Now that you have your vision, your motives, and your timetable laid out, you're ready to start drawing up an action plan for this project! The first step is to take a complete inventory of your ideas! Include every step that you're aware of, anything that you'll need to make it happen. This might include social media planning, email campaign concepts, marketing plans, print ideas, product development, manufacturing, networking, and anything else related to your project. Address each of these elements here:

_____

_____

_____

_____

_____

_____

_____

_____

_____

_____

_____

The Project Planner

The purpose of this planner is to organize all of the components listed on your 'idea throw-down'. For almost any project, you'll have multiple components – website development, sales, marketing, and so forth. As you research each area, you'll begin to find countless *great ideas* that you'll want to incorporate. A formatted Project Planner is available at TheSuccessProject.com for purchase, or you can use a lined journal of your choice! This is how I organize my planner:

Vision Statement

Start with a vision statement. Write yours in the front of your planner. This is your intention for the project, the future and ultimate goal of the business! In some cases, a vision statement can be summed up in a few words or it might be a few sentences.

As you develop your vision statement, consider how your project will make a difference in the world, how you will function within that picture, and how it will draw in others. Think beyond the basic functions of your business, and identify your secret sauce… the thing that makes your project special! What are you offering that sets you apart from the rest? This point will be beneficial in bringing others aboard and it will narrow your purpose, helping you identify the necessary components of your project plan.

Your Vision Statement:

_____

_____

_____

_____

_____

_____

_____

_____

_____

_____

_____

_____

_____

_____

_____

_____

_____

_____

Organize Your Planner

This is a great way to take a ton of ideas, and consolidate them into an organized format. If you're planning to write a formal business plan, this will be a great starting point.

At the front of your planner, create a list of project elements to serve as your planner's Table of Contents. This could include the areas just mentioned: product development, website, sales, marketing, each is a separate project element. Here's a sample to reference as you build your own project element list:

	Project Element
1	Research and Write Business Plan
2	Write an ebook
3	Develop corresponding web tutorial script
4	Expand web tutorial into Powerpoint presentation
5	Obtain domain name for project
6	Develop Website
7	Shoot Video Segments
8	Integrate video
9	Integrate membership component
10	Establish email campaign resources
11	Establish social media channels
12	Integrate social media marketing and campaigns

Once that table of contents is in place you can begin labeling chapter headings every several pages throughout the book leaving 5-10 pages for each element. Leave plenty of room for those project details!

Finally, add the details for each element. This will come through research and those little daily inspirations that often come without warning. Here you will organize them, and possibly give each item a timetable for completion. This will be your reference guide for this project! Keep that planner with you so that that you can record new ideas as they come in an organized, concise format. When you come across a great inspiration, record it under the corresponding chapter heading. In my own project planners I've included timetables, pictures, flowcharts, estimates, phone numbers, websites/resources, contacts, book resources, and storyboards - all categorized under each respective "project element"/chapter. Although you won't see all of the details from the start, this organized brainstorming process will certainly get your game plan started. As you work through your project details, you'll see where to fill in the blanks.

Refer to your planner as you develop your short-term goals. I generally stay on task with a written action item list based on those items from my project journal. Here's a little space to get the process started:

Section#	Project Element
1	
2	
3	
4	
5	
6	
7	
8	
9	
10	
11	
12	
13	

Declutter. Make Room for the Good Stuff

As mentioned, inspiration is everything. You can do anything that you've been inspired to do. You will be qualified for whatever purpose is given to you. But you must have clarity. You must be available to receive the instruction. You can be the vehicle. It's all about preparing your engine, cleansing your inner vessel, and allowing God to work through you. It may require some decluttering or perhaps a massive overhaul. You know what's necessary. You can start right now.

This decluttering process was written to help you identify your own toxic habits and remove them altogether. Think about the negative habits that influence the way your see yourself, as well as those that impact the important relationships in your life. Through the following introspections you can begin lightening your load and maximizing your effectiveness in each dimension of your life. Declutter, and make room for the good stuff!

Habit Replacement Plan

Research has proven that the best way to change a bad habit is to replace it. Start by identifying your ineffective habits, then identify an ideal replacement habit:

Clutter	Replacement Habit
ACTIONS	

Clutter	Replacement Habit
WORDS	

Clutter	Replacement Habit
THOUGHTS	

I believe that as we create a foundation for our vision, form quantifiable goals for the future, and properly cultivate our vision with positive thoughts and actions, we can be the vehicle to something truly amazing. Always start by seeking divine guidance and prepare yourself sufficiently to receive the answers. You will do it.

Works Cited

Alexander, Ronald, *The Power of Affirmations: How to Make Them Work for You*, www.RonaldAlexander.com

Benson, Ezra Taft– *Gifts and Expectations*, General Conference May, 1975 The Church of Jesus Christ of Latter-Day Saints. www.lds.org

Canfield, Jack. *Success Principles*. New York: HarperCollins Publishers, 2005.

Covey, Stephen. *The Seven Habits of Highly Effective People*. First Fireside Edition 1990.

Dalton, Elaine. Conversations Podcast, Episode 7. Mormonchannel.org

Dew, Sheri. *If Life Were Easy it Wouldn't Be Hard*. Salt Lake City: Deseret Book Company, 2005.

Holland, Jeffrey R .*Like a Broken Vessel*, General Conference October 2013, The Church of Jesus Christ of Latter-Day Saints. www.lds.org

Peale, Norman V. The Power of Positive Thinking: Prentice-Hall, Inc, 1952. First Fireside Edition: 2003

Uchdorf, Dieter F. *The Hope of God's Light*, General Conference April 2013, The Church of Jesus Christ of Latter-Day Saints. www.lds.org

Featured

Alison Faulkner — www.thealisonshow.com

Amie White - www.mydoterra.com/amiewhite

Andrea Faulkner Williams   - www.tubbytodd.com

Andrea Tagalog — paleobloks.com, fitnessbodysolutions.com

Calee Reed — caleereed.com

Collette Larsen - Larsenglobal.com

Dianna Barton — plumandsparrow.com

Elaine Dalton — LDS.org

Erica Smart — humblehilo.com

Gaila Mackenzie — drgaila.com

Heidi Andrews — www.fairybirds.com

Heather Balliet - www.amorologyweddings.com

Jamie Pyatt

Jennifer Sattley — carlsbadcravings.com

Jill Thomas - www.jillthomasphoto.com

Kari Rich — http://m.facebook.com/chef.rich.3

Katie Sabin — Instagram @justaddsunshine (Etsy.com)

Lauren Foulger - www.Humblehilo.com

Onjali Pettingill — Paper Kite Designs (Etsy.com)

Rebecca Forbush — Instagram @rebeccaforbushcreations

Sharlie Kaltenbach — sharliek.com

Shelley Smith - www.thehouseofsmiths.com

Sheri Dew - LDS.org

Susan Martinez

Read more about these inspiring individuals and others at

TheSuccessProject.com